FINANCING LAND ACQUISITION AND DEVELOPMENT

NATIONAL ASSOCIATION OF HOME BUILDERS

Financing Land Acquisition and Development
ISBN 0-86718-281-4
Library of Congress Catalog Card Number 87-61069

Copyright © 1987 by the
National Association of Home Builders of the United States
15th and M Streets, N.W.
Washington, D.C. 20005

All rights reserved. No part of this book may be reproduced or utilized in any form or by any means, electronic or mechanical, including photocopying and recording, or by any information storage and retrieval system without permission in writing from the publisher.

When ordering this publication, please provide the following information:

    Title
    ISBN 0-86718-281-4
    Price
    Quantity
    NAHB membership number (as it appears on the
       Builder or *Nation's Building News* label)
    Mailing address (including street number and zip code)

Contents

Acknowledgements 7

Introduction 9

1. Knowing Your Market 13

Importance of Market Analysis 13

Trends 14
    Changes in Household Composition 14
    Changing Lifestyles 15
    More Knowledgeable Consumers 15
    Changing Investment Value of Real Estate . . . 15
    Increase in Two-Income Families 15
    Population Shifts to the South and West 16
    Increasing Competition from a Wider Variety
      of Products 16
    Changes in the Ability to Afford Housing . . . 16

Responses to Trends 16

New Approaches to Market Analysis 17
    Use of Comparables from Other Cities 17

The Market Analysis Process 18
    Economic Base Analysis 18
    Market Analysis 18
    Buyer Profile 18
    Geographic Market Area Definition 18
    Supply Determination 18

Market Indicators 19
    Employment 19
    Population 20
    Income 20

Current Building Activity 20
    Building Permits 21
    Absorption of Space 21
    Vacancy Rates 21

Consumer Research 21
    Focus Groups 22
    Random Sample Surveys 22
    Feasibility 22

Summary 24

2. Finding the Land 29

Community Analysis 29
    Appraisers 29
    Newspapers 30
    Economic Surveys 30
    Windshield Survey 31
    Dodge Reports 31
    Real Estate Agents 31

Neighborhood Analysis 31
    Catalogues and Magazines 32
    Aerial Photographs 32
    Helicopter 32

Site Location 34
    Existing Single-Family Lots 34
    Undeveloped Parcels 34
    Multifamily Parcels 35
    Broker Services 35
    Miscellaneous Sources 36

Summary 37

3. Raw Land Analysis and Site Selection . 39

Site Factors 39
    Transportation 39
    Utilities 41
    Sewer and Water 41
    Size and Shape of Parcel 41

Topography 42
Soils 42
Vegetation 44
Easements and Encroachments 44
Deed Restrictions 44
Liens 45
Mineral Rights 47

Government Plans and Regulations 47
Comprehensive Plans 48
Zoning Ordinances 49
Subdivision Regulations 50
Building Codes 50

Value Analysis 50
Land Valuation Example 51

4. Organization for Acquisition and Sale 53

Sole Proprietorship 53

General Partnership 53
Avoiding Tax Problems 54

Corporation 54

Summary 55

5. Methods for Acquisition 57

Standard Land Purchase Contract 57

Contingency Contract 57

Option or Option Contract 57

Land Installment Contract 58

Phased Land Purchase Contract 58

Summary 58

6. Private Sector Financing Alternatives . 59

Financing Phases 59

Financing Land Acquisition 59
Purchase Money Mortgage 60
Purchase Option 60
Long-Term Lease Plus Option 60
Joint Venture 61
Interim Land Loans 61

Land Development Financing 61

Construction Financing 62
Sources of Construction Financing 62
Characteristics of Construction Financing . . . 63
Risks of Construction Lending 63
Loan Disbursements 63

The Take-Out Commitment 64
Commitment Duration 64
Commitment Rate 64
Commitment Cost 64
Special Commitment Terms 64
Sources of Commitment Funds 65

Interim Financing 65

Sale and Leaseback Transactions 65
Advantages 65
Disadvantages 66

Equity Financing 66
Joint Ventures 67
Syndications 68

7. Public Financing Alternatives 71

Revenue Bonds 71
Tax-Exempt Financing for
Single-Family Housing 71
Industrial Revenue Bonds for
Multifamily Housing 72
Summary 74

Housing Finance Agencies 74
Single-Family Programs 74
Multifamily Programs 75
Housing Rehabilitation and
Home Improvement Programs 76
Future of Housing Finance Agencies 76

Tax Increment Financing 76
Representative Statute [Illinois] 77
Application of TIF 80
Summary 81

Tax Abatement Financing 82
Summary 84

HUD Title 10 Programs 84
    Selection Criteria for Title 10 Housing 84
    Eligible Mortgagors and Mortgagees 85
    Mortgage Requirements, Terms and
        Fees Under Title 10 85
    The Title 10 Application Process 86

Special Districts 86
    Uses of Metropolitan Service Districts 86
    Powers of Metropolitan Service Districts 87
    Establishing a Metropolitan Service District . . . 87
    Bonds 88
    Other Considerations 88

8. Selecting a Lender and Preparing the Loan Application 93

Selecting the Lender 93

Types of Lending Institutions 94
    Commercial Banks 94
    Savings and Loan Associations 95
    Mutual Savings Banks 95
    Real Estate Investment Trusts 96

Packaging the Loan Submission 96
    Cover Letter 97
    Loan Summary 97
    The Borrower 97
    Market Data 97
    Project Data 97
    Financial Proformas 98
    Appendix 98

Loan Commitment and Closing 98

Summary 98

Appendix 99

5-A Standard Land Purchase Contract 101

5-B Option Contract 106

5-C Land Installment Contract 111

5-D Phased Land Purchase Contract 115

7-A Tax Increment Financing Statutes for Indiana,
    Minnesota, Ohio, California, and Florida   121

7-B Details of the Limitations on Qualified
    Redevelopment Bonds as Specified in the
    Tax Reform Act of 1986 127

8-A Application for a Land Acquisition and
    Development Loan 129

Acknowledgements

Financing Land Acquisition and Development represents the expertise of numerous financial, legal, tax, and land acquisition authorities. Each of them enjoys a close affiliation with the National Association of Home Builders; their contributions of time and knowledge are deeply appreciated.

Kenneth D. Bleakly, contributing author for Chapter 6, Private Sector Financing Alternatives, is director of real estate advisory services for the Denver office of Laventhol & Horwath, where he directs the firm's economic research activities for the Rocky Mountain area real estate industry. He is a featured speaker at NAHB land development seminars. Prior to joining Laventhol & Horwath, Bleakly was a research manager with Urban Systems Research and Engineering in Boston, and a research associate with the Center for Urban Policy Research at Rutgers University. He is co-author of *Urban Homesteading* and *Methods of Housing Analysis* (Center for Urban Policy Research, New Brunswick, NJ).

Miriam Evans, contributing author for Chapter 6, Private Sector Financing Alternatives and Chapter 7, Public Sector Financing Alternatives, is a manager in the real estate advisory practice of Laventhol & Horwath in Denver. In that capacity, she provides consulting services to home builders, commercial developers, and public agencies in the Rocky Mountain region. Her areas of expertise include market analysis, financial feasibility, and financial deal structuring.

Gregory W. Hummel, contributing author for Chapter 7, Public Sector Financing Alternatives, is an attorney and partner with the Chicago law firm of Rudnick & Wolfe. He specializes in real estate law and practice with concentration in zoning, development, construction, and financing law. Hummel is a featured speaker at NAHB land development seminars. He is a member of the American Bar Association, where he serves as chairman of the Committee on Construction Contracts and Architects' Contracts and as co-chairman of the National Institute on Construction Law and Practice. He is associate director of the Board of Directors of the Home Builders Association of Greater Chicago, and is a contributing author for the *Construction Law Institute Handbook* (Illinois Institute of Technology) and *Illinois Real Estate Forms* (in preparation, Aspen Publications, Inc.).

Christopher C. Inman is author of Chapter 2, Finding the Land and Chapter 3, Raw Land Analysis and Site Selection. He is president of Inman Homes, Inc. in Albuquerque, builder/developers of single- and multifamily homes. Inman has taught finance and real estate at the University of New Mexico, and previously served as senior vice president, administrative services division, with First National Bank in Albuquerque. He is an NAHB director, a director and past president of the Central New Mexico Home Builders Association, and a director of the Home Owners Warranty Council of New Mexico. He also serves on NAHB's Land Developers Committee.

David Jensen Associates, Inc., author of Chapter 1, Knowing Your Market, is a multidisciplinary consulting firm headquartered in Denver, specializing in land planning, economic analysis, landscape architecture, and design. Contributing staff include David R. Jensen, president of the company, NAHB seminar speaker, and member of NAHB's Land Developers Committee; James R. Lincoln, Jr. (now president of The Lincoln Company in Denver), Jennifer Quinn, and Denise Katz, who provided writing and editing assistance; and Pat Stiffler, who provided production support. David Jensen Associates, Inc. is the author of several NAHB land development publications, including *Community Applications of Density, Design and Cost; Community Design Guidelines: Responding to a Changing Market;* and *How to Win at the Zoning Table.*

James H. Lunn authored Chapter 4, Organization for Acquisition and Sale; Chapter 5, Methods for Acquisition; and Chapter 8, Selecting a Lender and Preparing the Loan Application. He is president of Lunn Limited, a real estate development and construction firm in Chicago. He was formerly executive vice president of Lyons Realty Group in Chicago, a savings and loan service corporation specializing in land acquisition, development, and construction. Lunn also served as vice president with Talman Savings and Loan in Chicago, where he coordinated the management and disposition of real estate owned by Talman. He is a former director of marketing and sales for Larwin, Inc. and Kaufman & Broad, Inc. Lunn is a member of the Home Builders Association of Greater Chicago, and has been a featured speaker at NAHB land development seminars.

Lunn wishes to acknowledge the encouragement and assistance of his attorney, Marianne D. Yacobellis, a land acquisition and development specialist and partner in the firm of Cellucci & Yacobellis, Naperville, IL.

Larry Mayer, president of Larry Mayer & Company, provided guidance in the development of *Financing Land Acquisition and Development.* His firm, with offices in Chicago and Boca Raton, FL, specializes in land acquisition, development, and brokerage. Mayer is a member of NAHB's Land Developers Committee and recently chaired its Subcommittee on Land Acquisition and Development Finance. A life member of NAHB, Mayer has been a featured speaker at NAHB land development seminars. He is also a member of the Home Builders Association of Greater Chicago and the Northern Illinois Home Builders Association.

William C. Nussbaum, contributing author for Chapter 7, Public Sector Financing Alternatives, is an attorney with the Washington, D.C. law firm of Lane and Edson, P.C., specializing in real estate development, construction, and finance law. Nussbaum is a member of the Illinois State Bar, the District of Columbia Bar, and the American Bar Association. He is a co-author of *How to Protect Against a Tenant's Default Under a Commercial Lease* (The Practical Real Estate Lawyer, March 1985).

W. Travis Porter, III is a contributing author for Chapter 6, Private Sector Financing Alternatives and Chapter 7, Public Sector Financing Alternatives. He is executive vice president of Powe, Porter and Alphin, P.A. in Durham, NC, specializing in housing and business law. He has served as general counsel to the North Carolina Home Builders Association, the Home Builders Association of Durham and Chapel Hill, and the North Carolina Housing Finance Agency. Porter is a member of the Board of Trustees of the University of North Carolina at Chapel Hill, and has been an adjunct professor of business law in the Graduate School of Business at Duke University. He is a member of the North Carolina Bar and the American Bar Association.

James L. Stuart, contributing author for Chapter 6, Private Sector Financing Alternatives and Chapter 7, Public Sector Financing Alternatives, is a partner in the law firm of Moore and Van Allen (Raleigh, NC office), specializing in construction and business law. His clients include the North Carolina Housing Finance Agency and the North Carolina Home Builders Association. Stuart is a former adjunct instructor at the University of North Carolina School of Law, and is a former assistant attorney general with the North Carolina Department of Justice. He is a member of the North Carolina Bar and the American Bar Associations.

Authors Gregory W. Hummel and William C. Nussbaum wish to acknowledge the contributions of David Goss, Mark Gershon, Robert Hirsch, and Peter Ross to Chapter 7, Public Sector Financing Alternatives.

Financing Land Acquisition and Development was prepared under the direction of the 1985-86 NAHB Land Developers Committee, Dale DeHarpport, chairman; Mark Tipton, vice chairman; and Larry Mayer, chairman of the Land Acquisition and Development Finance Subcommittee, It was produced under the general direction of Kent W. Colton, NAHB executive vice president, by the following staff members:

William D. Ellingsworth, Senior Staff Vice President, Public Affairs
Denise L. Darling, Staff Vice President, Publishing Services
Michael F. Shibley, Director, Land Use and Environmental Affairs
Susan D. Bradford, Director, Publications
David Rhodes, Art Director
Karen Haas Smith, Editor

Introduction

There is no special magic to securing financing for land development. Lenders and investors need good investment opportunities as much as developers need sources of financing. Lenders will judge investment opportunities based on the estimated rate of return on investment and the level of perceived risk. If your proposal offers better money-making potential than the competition's, you have a good chance of getting your project funded.

Keep in mind that much of the information lenders require to evaluate an application for project financing is information that you need, too, in order to properly analyze your own potential for profit. Even small-scale developers need to go through the process of market analysis, which is explained in Chapter One of this book, "Knowing Your Market." Preparation of a formal market analysis may not be necessary, but thinking through all of the points covered in Chapter One is important.

Understanding the economic base of the community is sometimes simple—as in the case of a farming community, or one dominated by a few manufacturing firms. But getting a good handle on the total economic environment surrounding your proposed venture can be difficult. Employment, population, and income statistics can tell you what trends have been in the past, but you need to know what is likely to happen to the local economy in the future. Economic forecasting is an art in itself; developers need to tap all the sources of local business information available to them.

National economic trends affect the housing industry immediately and very strongly, because interest rate fluctuations have a significant impact on housing affordability. The housing market tends to be cyclical, expanding and contracting regularly as interest rates fall and rise. While these trends are becoming increasingly difficult to predict, organizations such as the National Association of Home Builders publish regular economic forecasts for the housing industry that should be required reading for developers.

The second step in market analysis is comparison of supply and demand. While this may seem to be an obvious step, it is easy to overlook in some circumstances. In a booming development market where everything that is built seems to sell right away, there is a temptation to assume that demand will remain very strong. It is important to remember that market saturation will occur at some point, and you want to make sure the market will remain strong when your completed project goes on the market. Supply and demand determination is especially important in very active markets.

The final phase of market analysis is developing a buyer profile, which, again, need not be a formal process in the case of smaller-scale projects, but is always necessary. Whenever you offer a product on the speculative market, you need to know the needs and preferences of your potential buyer. Think about the lifestyle, taste, and financial circumstances of your targeted buyer. Make very sure that you know what design options appeal to this buyer. You will learn more about your market as you search for possible sites and make comparisons among them.

Chapter Two, "Finding the Land," suggests a number of techniques for researching communities and neighborhoods. Much of the work is routine and time-consuming—reading newspapers, magazines, and housing industry reports; researching public documents; driving the area; interviewing appraisers, bankers, engineers, city planners, home buyers; and so on. While you may be tempted to skip some of these activities, there is no substitute for the first-hand knowledge that personal investigation can provide.

The process of evaluating potential land development sites involves even more investigation. Chapter Three, "Raw Land Analysis and Site Selection," covers the evaluation of site factors, governmental land use controls, as well as land value analysis. Overlooking issues at this point can be a critical mistake. Be sure you thoroughly investigate all of the site factors, and have the benefit of excellent engineering advice. Also check all governmental regulations and plans, so that no land use restrictions take you by surprise. Then buy the land.

If your development plans face public opposition, try to establish communication with critics rather than taking an adversarial attitude. Address the issues raised by opponents in a straightforward manner, and strive to project a public image of yourself as a competent professional who is concerned about how the proposed development will affect the community. Simply denying the validity of complaints about your project is not enough; you must show how and why your critics are mistaken. Getting angry or defensive will make you seem unprofessional.

Chapters Four and Five briefly cover accounting and legal aspects of land acquisition, giving you background that will help you to work effectively with your accountant and attorney. Chapter Four, "Organization for Acquisition and Sale," outlines possible ways of organizing your land development company. Chapter Five, "Methods for Acquisition," explains common types of land acquisition contracts. These arrangements depend to some degree on the outcome of negotiations with other parties, including potential partners, investors, and land sellers. The developer must remain personally involved in these negotiations, to be certain that his/her interests are properly represented and the outcome of negotiations is reflected properly in the legal arrangements.

Chapter Six, "Private Sector Financing Alternatives," and Chapter Seven, "Public Financing Alternatives," give developers detailed information on the financing options available for various phases of land development and types of projects. Developers typically finance each phase of land development projects separately. The four phases of financing for a typical residential project are:

- Land acquisition financing
- Land development financing
- Construction financing
- Interim financing

Relatively few major institutional lenders are involved in land acquisition financing. In the absence of conventional financing, the developer is faced with five means of alternative financing:

- Purchase money mortgage
- Purchase option
- Long-term lease plus option
- Joint venture
- Interim land loans

Chapter Six explains each of these in detail.

Loans for land development usually represent a first lien on the property, and involve interest rates 3 to 4 points above prime. Among the institutional lenders, commercial banks and certain savings and loan institutions are most involved in land development financing. Lenders often are willing to lend 70 to 80 percent of the appraised value of the finished lots, as long as that amount does not exceed the costs associated with land acquisition and construction. Land development financing typically covers site preparation, installation of infrastructure, consultants' fees, and other soft costs. Chapter Six lists the information lenders often require in land development applications; Chapter Eight gives additional guidance on preparing loan applications.

While the primary focus of this book is financing land acquisition and development, many institutional lenders are active in financing the construction phase of residential development as well. If the lender does not know you, you will have to provide documentary evidence of your technical and financial ability to complete the proposed project. Information on banking relationships, creditworthiness, and references from those who have done business with you often are requested. Moreover, lenders often require developers to pledge their personal assets to ensure the project's successful completion, particularly if you have established a "one-shot" corporation for the development of a single project. In addition, usually you will be required to obtain a performance bond as well as a labor and materials bond.

Once the loan agreement is signed, both lender and developer must follow a strict loan disbursement process. Funds are made available as work progresses. Lenders conduct frequent inspections to make certain that the work is proceeding according to plan, and the funds are being disbursed properly.

Lenders of construction funding for residential properties often require a take-out commitment, which is an agreement by the builder to assume the permanent loan directly if the house is not sold within one year of the commitment date. Under this contingency, the builder still faces the problem of selling the house, but is responsible for only a monthly payment rather than immediate repayment of the full amount of the construction loan, and the construction lender receives full payment. A wide variety of such take-out commitments is available to residential developers. The major differences are in loan duration, interest rates, and costs. The principal sources of take-out funds are thrift institutions, commercial banks, and mortgage bankers.

Interim financing is sometimes necessary to pay off the construction loan and finance carrying costs until the sale of the units. Chapter Six discusses situations where interim financing may be helpful.

Alternatives to debt financing such as sale/leaseback transactions, equity financing, joint ventures and syndications are covered in detail in Chapter Six.

Chapter Seven explores the many options for public financing, including tax-exempt revenue bond programs, tax abatement financing, HUD Title 10 programs, and special assessment districts. Tax-exempt bonds fund state and local housing agency programs that traditionally have served as a source of single-family mortgages, placing several hundred million dollars worth of loans each year to low- and moderate-income single-family home buyers and to developers of multifamily housing for low- and moderate-income tenants. Tax abatement programs encourage socially desirable development by offering tax breaks. Special assessment districts are often used to finance infrastructure (roads, water, sewer) services needed for private housing development.

The relatively new Tax Increment Financing (TIF) programs are also explained in detail in Chapter Seven. Most often used for larger, mixed-use projects, TIF programs permit developers to leverage the tax revenue increases expected to result from a project in defraying some of the initial development costs. Chapter Seven includes a detailed discussion of the Illinois TIF statute, and the appendix gives the highlights of the TIF programs in several other states to familiarize the developer with some of the complexities involved in these programs. A developer interested in exploring the possibility of TIF financing should consult an attorney familiar with local law.

Chapter Eight, "Selecting a Lender and Preparing the Loan Application," offers practical advice about dealing with lenders. The chapter gives basic information about the lending industry, explaining the services and capabilities of such diverse lending institutions as commercial banks, savings and loan associations, mutual savings banks, and real estate investment trusts. A comprehensive section on packaging the loan submission describes the elements of a typical loan submission package and gives offers on loan negotiation. The appendix includes a sample loan application form, which is a useful reference for the reader.

The material contained herein is not to be construed as legal advice or opinion. The authors, editor, and publisher do not assume responsibility for the accuracy or completeness of these materials.

Chapter One

Knowing Your Market

This introductory chapter provides basic background information that will be helpful in reading and using the remainder of the book.

Importance of Market Analysis

Knowing your market is essential to the development process. The overall development plan is based on market information and its relationship to physical, financial, and political conditions. Figure 1.1 is a graphic representation of the factors involved in the development process and their interrelationships. For example, the diagram shows:

- Political or regulatory requirements have at least two effects: they establish standards for the physical development, and they respond to market factors.
- The physical aspect of the development must conform to public standards, and form the basis for determining construction costs.
- The market analysis is sensitive to the political environment and provides a basis for design.

The development plan is generated in response to all of these various factors. Market analysis is an essential part of the preliminary planning process.

Financing land acquisition and development is a specialized field. Lenders and investors have become both sophisticated and cautious; they generally require a formal market analysis as a basis for assessing risk. Unless the project is small and the builder has an established track record, the lender will require a formal analysis prepared by an experienced market consulting firm.

Builders need to perform preliminary analyses to decide whether they should pursue a project. This chapter gives basic guidance on preliminary market analysis techniques, and can help you evaluate proposals you may later request from market evaluation consultants.

Market studies indicate project feasibility and influence land use allocation and product design. They are an up-front cost, but the cost is repaid in risk reduction and in project efficiency and marketability. They should be done well and completely.

The objectives of market analysis vary by project. Some common objectives include:

- Determining project feasibility
- Forecasting market absorption rates
- Determining marketable project designs and features
- Developing a marketing plan
- Providing documentation to support zoning or annexation permit requests
- Providing documentation for inclusion in financing applications

Typical products of market analysis include:

- Background studies for land use allocation and planning
- Recommendations for highest and best use of land
- Identification of the most marketable products (single-family, townhomes, condominiums)
- Identification of the most marketable amenities
- Recommendations for product pricing
- Recommendations for project size
- Proposed schedule for development timing and phasing

Comprehensive market reports also examine physical, social and governmental factors that could present potential constraints to development, such as site characteristics, zoning laws, environmental concerns,

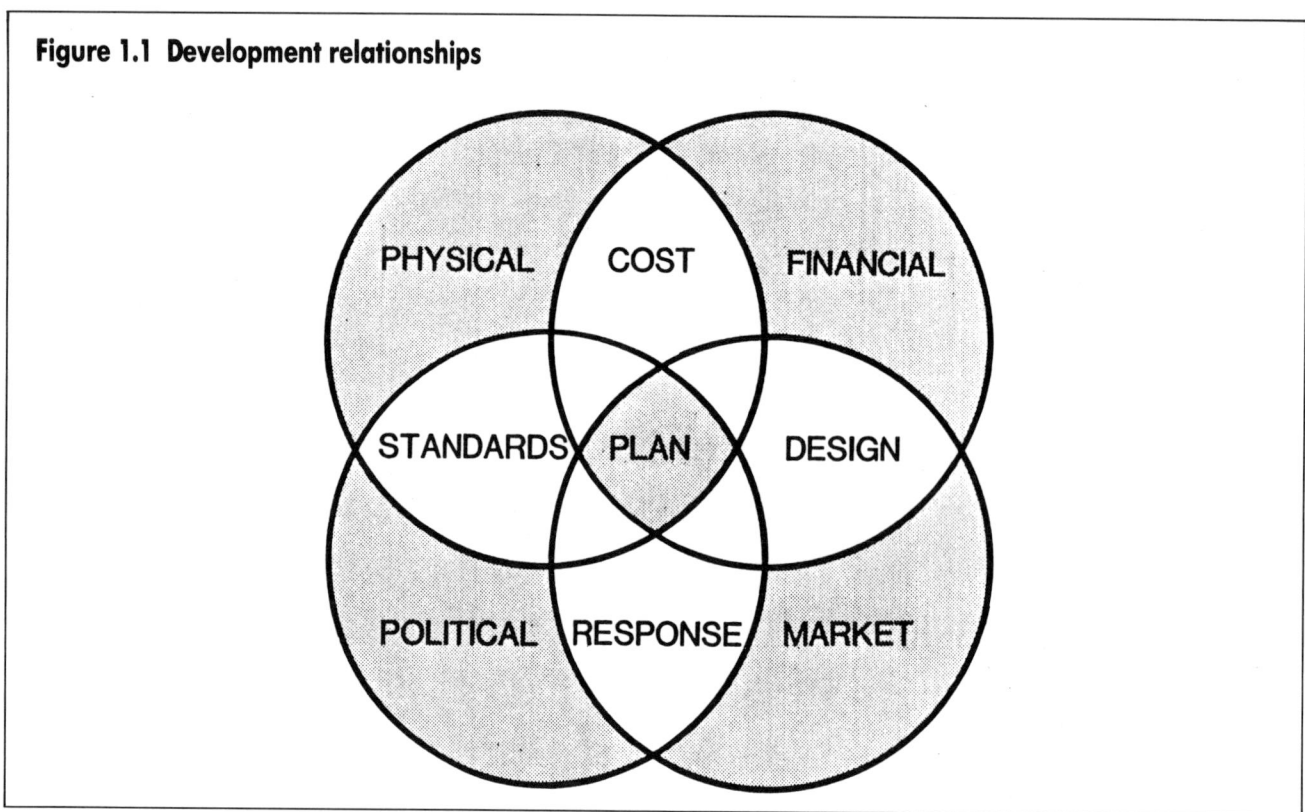

Figure 1.1 Development relationships

taxes, building codes, permit requirements and community interests. Chapter Two, "Finding the Land," and Chapter Three, "Raw Land Analysis and Site Selection," provide additional guidance regarding other potential development constraints, including access, traffic, and the availability of utilities.

Trends

Real estate markets are influenced by and respond to social trends. These include:

- Changes in household composition
- Changing lifestyles
- Increasing consumer knowledge
- Changing status of homes as an investment
- Increase in two-income households
- Movement of population concentrations
- Increasing competition from a wider variety of products
- Changes in the ability to afford housing

Changes in Household Composition

Not long ago, the traditional family had a working husband, stay-at-home wife, and one or more children. As recently as 1970, traditional families comprised more than 70 percent of all households. Traditional families now account for less than 20 percent of all households.[1] Another important change that has occurred over the last 15 years is the decrease in the size of the average household to less than three persons.

During the 1970s, market analysts focused on four major segments of the home-buying public: young families, mature families, "empty-nesters," and retirees. Because of changes in household composition, the number of categories has expanded to include singles, "never-nesters," unrelated individuals living in groups, single-parent families, and two-income families.

In January 1985 *Multi-Housing News* acknowledged changing household composition and lifestyles in a humorous but perceptive "Target Market Guide" column. The editors identified:

"Yappies"—Young aspiring professionals
"Yuppies"—Young upwardly mobile professionals
"Treaders"—Born to rent
"Trendies"—Creative individualists
"Grumpies"—Grown-up mature persons
"Grampies"—Retired couples on fixed incomes

The point of these identifications was to show stratifications in the housing market, and to indicate differences in consumer needs and expectations related to household configuration and lifestyle.

Changing Lifestyles

Geographic location, income, occupation, age, mobility and home ownership status all affect lifestyle. The shift away from traditional households has stimulated a new diversity in lifestyles and housing needs. A wider variety of housing product types is demanded, and an increased need to define the characteristics of target market segments is apparent.

Retirement housing emerged as a major market opportunity in the mid-1980s due to the growing proportion of elderly persons in the U.S. population. In June 1985, *Builder* magazine offered the following analysis of three segments of the retirement housing market based on age and fitness characteristics, and suggested types of projects that could meet their diverse needs:

The "Go-Go's": "Young" retirees, 65 to 74 years old. They are active, independent and want to enjoy their newly acquired leisure.

The "Slow-Go's": People between 75 and 85 years old who are starting to slow down, but aren't ready for the rocking chair yet. This is the prime market for congregate housing (see below).

The "No-Go's": After 85 most folks have slowed down. They need services—from personal help with dressing, bathing and other daily functions, to skilled nursing care.

Three distinct types of housing would meet the diverse needs of the different sectors of the retirement market:

Active retirement communities span a range of projects from entire new towns to modest subdivisions, but all require residents to be over a certain age, usually about 50. Most offer a range of recreational opportunities similar to those offered in a resort community. These projects attract active retirees (65 to 74 years old), and do not provide health care facilities.

Congregate living is an updated version of the boarding house. Residents have their own apartments, equipped with at least one bedroom and a kitchen, but one or more of the daily meals is served in a common dining room. Weekly maid service, transportation and organized activities usually are included in the rent, but most congregate projects do not provide health care services.

Life care communities are usually campus-type projects that provide for nearly every contingency in an older person's life, including health care. Life care residents are usually over 85.

More Knowledgeable Consumers

Through the early 1980s high interest rates affected the ability of potential home purchasers to qualify for mortgages. This caused consumers to delay home purchases. Because the average age of first-time homebuyers has increased, the homebuyer is more knowledgeable about what is available, and has a definite housing preference. This places pressure on the home builder to supply a variety of competitive products that meet the needs of the identified market segments within a geographic area.

Changing Investment Value of Real Estate

About 50 years ago the United States introduced government policies and tax incentives to promote the homebuilding industry. Since that time the majority of American families have viewed housing not merely as shelter, but as a major financial investment and status symbol. However, during recent decades, increasing housing costs—particularly financing costs—have made homeownership unattainable for a growing proportion of households. With the reduction in inflation and price appreciation in the early 1980s, homeownership lost some of its attraction as a primary investment vehicle (a hedge against inflation). However, the basic demand for shelter and consumer desires for comfort and convenience continued to assure demand for new housing. More recently, the economic cycle has been on an upswing, and interest rates have declined. These trends have meant that the cost of new housing is again affordable to larger numbers of households.

Increase in Two-Income Families

Although women first began entering the workforce in large numbers during World War II, it was the women's movement of the late 1960s and early 1970s that created greater opportunities for women. In many families, the presence of women in the workforce has now become a matter of household economics rather than social change. The consumer price index in the United States rose by over 48 percent between 1979 and 1985 alone.[2] Many American families need two incomes to maintain a lifestyle previously possible on one income.

The trend toward two-income families has many implications for developers. Where both spouses work, low-maintenance, smaller homes with timesaving features have appeal. Innovative developers also offer amenities geared to two-income famiies, such as child-care and recreation facilities.

Population Shifts to the South and West

The Southern and "sunbelt" states have seen substantial population growth in the last 15 years. While these regions will probably continue to grow, the areas that are projected to have the fastest growth in the next 15 years are the East South Central States (Mississippi, Alabama, Tennessee and Kentucky), the West South Central States (Louisiana, Arkansas, Oklahoma and Texas) and the Mountain States (New Mexico, Arizona, Colorado, Utah, Nevada, Wyoming, Idaho and Montana). Housing demand in these new growth areas will increase in the near future, particularly for higher density homes. Eventually, as the younger "in-migrants" mature and have families, larger homes will be needed, while retirees in these areas will be "moving down" to smaller, more convenient homes.[3]

Increasing Competition from a Wider Variety of Products

In an environment where lifestyles, households, and consumers are changing rapidly, developers have been innovative in offering products to suit the changing needs and wants of consumers. As a result, a wide variety of competitive products is offered in the housing market. The traditional single-family detached home on a large lot is now supplemented by zero-lot-line homes, patio or garden homes, townhomes, condominiums and other housing types. All of these products compete with each other. As the market continues to change, developers will need to find unserved segments and serve them in increasingly innovative ways.

Changes in the Ability to Afford Housing

Affordability, the last item on the list of important trends affecting the housing market, is perhaps the most crucial.

Shifts in the relative buying power of home purchasers over the last three decades have narrowed the market considerably. The two primary culprits are:

- Inflation—Increased land and building costs
- Interest rates—Progressive increases through 1983

The rate of increase in building costs has slowed, but the rate of housing price appreciation has also slowed. And income increases have diminished. The shifts in buying power have been offset somewhat by changes in lending criteria. More permissive rules for buyer qualification and more flexible financing techniques were developed in response to high interest rates in the late 1970s and early 1980s. High foreclosure rates were the eventual result, and in October 1985, during a period of descending interest rates, qualification requirements began to tighten.

But adversity is not despair. Opportunities remain in the marketplace. Analysts can find them and responsive design and pricing can exploit them.

Responses to Trends

The homebuilding industry has responded to changing consumer needs and preferences through shifts in product design and mix, and by offering new amenities. Figure 1.2 illustrates the changing mixes of single-family and multifamily housing over the last 15 years. Except for the early 1970s, multifamily units have accounted for 50 percent or less of the total dwelling units authorized by permit each year. Other recent responses to consumer trends include:

- Smaller houses on smaller lots, or higher density multifamily units that offer a more affordable product.
- Patio homes and condominiums that require less maintenance than conventional homes.
- Housing features that are designed for convenience and time-saving.
- Recreational amenities are often included in new developments: golf courses, jogging paths, swimming pools, and meeting, game or hobby rooms.
- Residential developments aimed at particular demographic market segments, including the elderly.
- Child-care centers for single parents and two-income families.

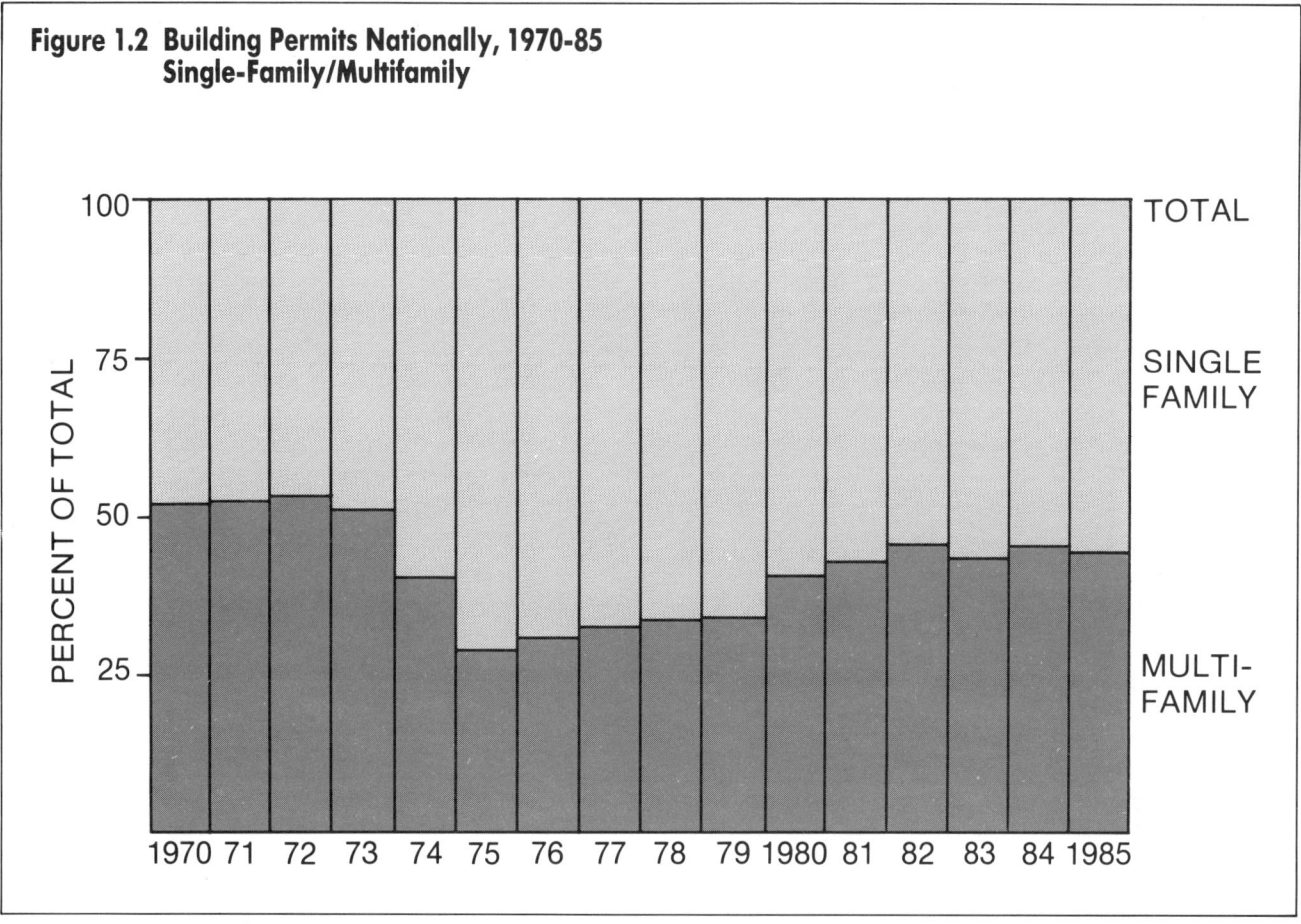

Figure 1.2 Building Permits Nationally, 1970-85
Single-Family/Multifamily

- Housing with built-in rentals, where zoning permits, creating the opportunity for income to offset increased housing costs.
- High-rises that accommodate increased densities in response to higher land costs and lifestyle adjustments.

As builders respond to the needs of target market segments, they will find buyers impressed with their products. Housing can be designed to sell as well as to be lived in.[4]

New Approaches to Market Analysis

Market investigations have become increasingly sophisticated, due in part to the availability of more demographic information through a variety of sources, including computerized data bases.

Census data once provided most demographic information—such as age, income, marital status and education levels—but now updated and detailed information can be obtained from a variety of sources. Many state agencies, local governments and private research firms provide abundant demographic detail about the areas within their purview.

City, county, and regional planning departments collect particularly valuable information and are aware of trends and future projects. *Sales and Marketing Management* magazine is a frequently quoted source of market and income data. Many other trade and specialized periodicals offer market insights. These and other information sources are listed at the end of this chapter.

Demographic information and other types of data such as household sizes, housing starts, employment levels and competitive inventories have been integrated into computerized data bases. Though these data bases can be time-consuming to develop, information can be quickly and inexpensively retrieved once on-line. Constant updating is required, but once the data base is set up, this task also takes relatively little time.

Some data bases are available on a subscription basis. The economics department of a major local bank, for example, may provide data for the occasional user on a subscription basis.

Use of Comparables from Other Cities

As real estate markets become more competitive, developers are becoming more innovative. When proposing a new product, it is customary to illustrate feasibility by citing comparable projects. If a product is new to a geographic market, comparable products from other cities of a similar economic and demographic composition are useful.[5] The services of a multi-disciplinary land planning and urban design firm with a national clientele can be helpful in proposal development under these circumstances.

The Market Analysis Process

The identification of a product and a target buyer profile is the result of the progression shown in Figure 1.3.

Economic Base Analysis

An understanding of the economic base of the community or metropolitan area is essential in determining the validity of growth forecasts and in identification of changes or cycles in the economy. The economic base analysis identifies important indicators, including employment, population, income and age distribution.

Market Analysis

The actual market analysis is a comparison of supply and demand. This is the process through which we identify competition and estimate the quantity of housing that will be required, by category.

Buyer Profile

The basic market question is always, "Who buys?" Many of the market analysis techniques we describe are focused on deriving buyer profiles.

Development of buyer profiles and supply and demand analyses enable the developer to identify the target market, and begin to define the characteristics of the product, its pricing, and possible project phasing.

Geographic Market Area Definition

An early step in any real estate market analysis is geographic market area definition. The primary considerations in defining a geographic market area are access, physical boundaries, commuting patterns, and location of competition. Sometimes jurisdictional boundaries that conform closely to primary considerations are used. Examples of these are census tracts or traffic zones, municipalities or school districts. Other factors to consider in market area definition include transportation networks, employment locations, commuting patterns, topography, and neighborhood characteristics. Another important information source is a recent aerial photograph (discussed in greater detail in Chapter 2).

Certain land uses have specific market area characteristics. Shopping center market areas are determined by commuting patterns and by driving times, as well as the considerations mentioned above. Office and industrial market areas can be influenced by development propensities within an area. These include visibility; surrounding land uses; natural resources; government policies or incentives for development; zoning; compatibility with other enterprises; type and quantity of the labor pool; traffic volumes; airport, rail and highway access; availability of water, sewer and utilities; and proximity to services such as courts, hospitals and financial institutions.

Supply Determination

Within the market area, it is important to identify the present and potential housing supply that might be in competition with a proposed project. An inventory of potentially competitive subdivisions is an important step. The resale market should also be evaluated. Although it adds nothing to the inventory, a large supply of homes in the resale market can absorb a substantial portion of projected housing demand.

A competitive inventory analysis evaluates the supply of housing within a defined geographic market area. A basic inventory provides an overview of housing conditions. It provides answers to questions such as:

- How many housing units exist?
- What types are they?
- What are the vacancy rates?
- What are the prices?
- Who are the buyers?

Comparing existing supply and vacancy rates with household growth projections will provide a quantification of annual housing demand.

A more comprehensive competitive inventory can focus on a particular product type and should be performed after

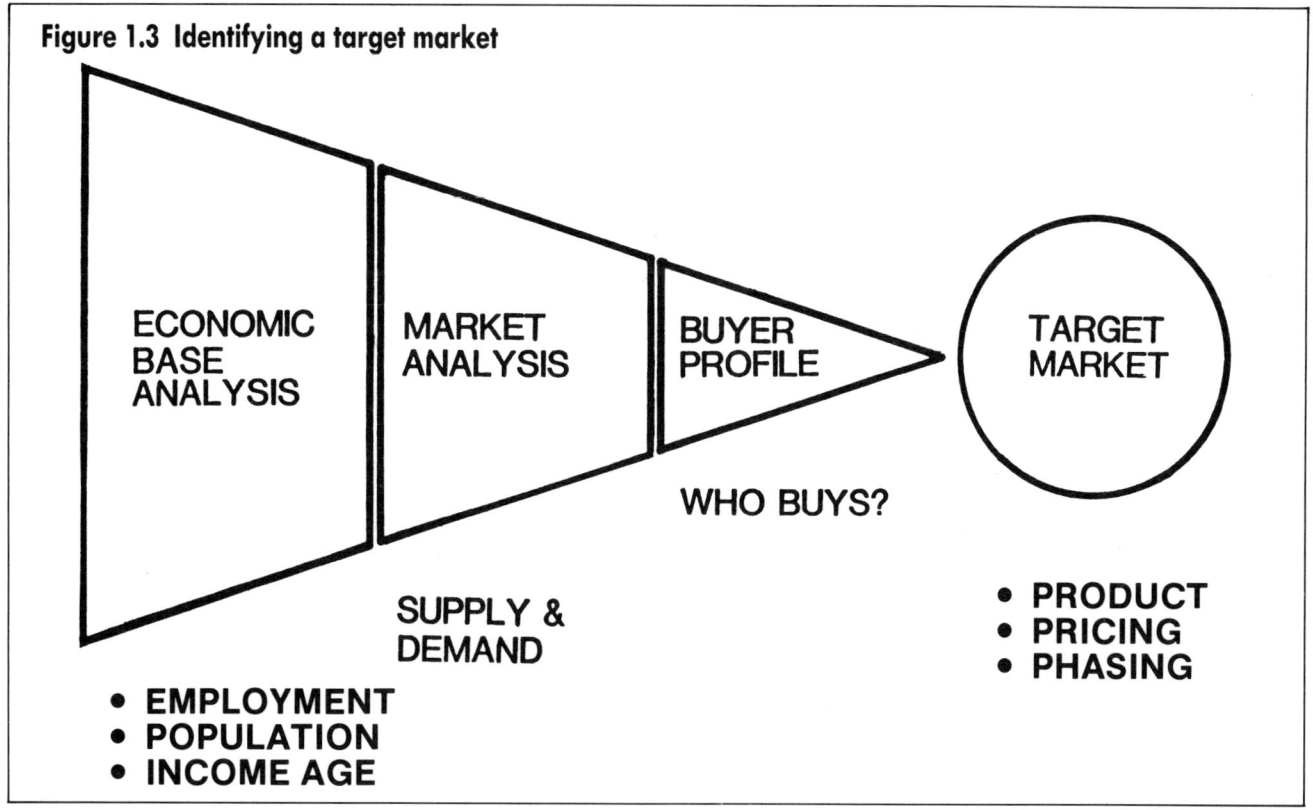

Figure 1.3 Identifying a target market

a target market and/or product type is identified. This competitive inventory will concentrate on current new housing projects. After projects are identified, they are visited, sales personnel are interviewed, and the following data are gathered:

- Project name
- Developer
- Location
- Style
- Number of units
- Mix of units
- Sales start
- Units sold
- Prices/lease rates
- Amenities
- Options
- Future plans and schedule

The foregoing data will help in determining features, prices, absorption rates and the target market for a planned project.

The competitive inventory in conjunction with other market and economic data will enable an analyst to determine whether current projects are satisfying market demand, creating an oversupply, or only partially fulfilling a need within the market area.

Market Indicators

From economic base analysis to buyer profile identification, the market analyst uses a variety of market indicators, including: employment trends, characteristics and forecasts; population characteristics, including possible seasonal variations; income levels and trends; and a variety of local phenomena that indicate supply and demand—such as identification of current building activity, building permit rates, certificates of occupancy, vacancy rates and absorption on a project-by-project basis.

Employment

Employment data can indicate an area's stability and growth potential, and characterize the existing and future labor force, which in turn point to the types of development needed based on community income and lifestyles.

Employment usually is analyzed in two categories: basic and non-basic. Industries that supply goods for consumption outside of the producing area are the source of basic employment. Non-basic employment is provided by businesses that support basic industries and the local community.[6] An understanding of the components of basic employment within an area is fundamental to determining that area's growth potential. Positive growth of basic industry is an indication of a strong economy and growth potential. A new or proposed basic industry also will stimulate growth in non-basic support industries.

A measure called the locational quotient can be used to

determine whether an industry is basic or non-basic. The locational quotient is found by dividing the percentage of local employment in a given industry by the percentage of national employment in the same industry. A locational quotient above 1.00 shows an industry to be basic; below 1.00 an industry is non-basic.

For example, if manufacturing of furniture and fixtures employs 4.6 percent of the wage and salary work force in the nation, and the percentage employed locally is 6.9, the locational quotient is 1.50 (6.9 divided by 4.6). This indicates that the industry generates basic employment.

Types of industries within the market area also can be classified according to Standard Industrial Classification (SIC) Codes. Typical SIC industry types are agricultural; mining; construction; manufacturing; transportation and public utilities; wholesale and retail trade; finance, real estate and insurance; services; and government.

Analysis of employment growth by industry and occupation indicates the types of facilities that will be required by new businesses and the categories of homebuyers who will be employed. Employment is also reported by occupation: professional, technical and managerial; clerical; sales; services; processing; machine trade; etc. This breakdown is particularly useful in analyzing housing demand in terms of buyer characteristics.

Population

Population counts and projections provide the basic measure of demand for housing within a defined market area. The analyst should distinguish between permanent and seasonal population. Population growth is the sum of natural increase and migration. Natural increase is the net sum of births over deaths. Migration can be positive or negative, depending on whether more people are moving in or out of an area.

Market analysts sometimes can obtain useful models for population forecasting from government agencies such as school districts and city planning departments, and private sector companies such as public utilities and telephone companies.

Income

Personal or household income distribution and its probable change over time help determine the degree of housing affordability in a given market. Income distribution by income category—as opposed to analysis based on median income—is important because there are differences in expenditure patterns at different income levels.

Housing price affordability in relation to income can be calculated based on Federal National Mortgage Association (Fannie Mae) criteria. As revised in October 1985, Fannie Mae rules required that the monthly mortgage payments of buyers seeking a 90 percent loan do not exceed 25 percent of their gross monthly income, and no more than 33 percent of their income when added to other installment debt. Previously, these figures were 28 percent and 35 percent, respectively.

After affordable housing prices have been calculated for income levels within the market area, a comparison can be made to the prices of homes actually purchased. This analysis can indicate whether homebuyers are purchasing at a price level equal to, above, or below their potential purchasing power. If they are buying below their potential purchasing power, market opportunities may exist because of a lack of available housing in appropriate price ranges.

The income distribution of households within a market area affects retail demand calculations. Lower-income households spend a larger proportion of household income on food and other necessities, while households in higher income categories spend a larger amount on discretionary purchases, savings and investments. These differences in expenditure patterns can have important consequences for the types of retail development appropriate to a given area.

Current Building Activity

Analysis of building activity in a market area aids a developer in characterizing the market and spotting the competition. The developer can obtain new construction information through local planning offices or building departments. Another way to gauge new construction activity is to perform a "windshield survey"—driving through a market area and recording the location and type of construction activity. Most construction sites post relevant information such as the names and phone numbers of developers, designers, finance sources and contractors, which can be used as the basis for more in-depth research.

Brisk construction activity can indicate a healthy market, but builders must be cautious in their assessment.

Overbuilding is often the result of a rush to capitalize on a trend that began as an opportunity but ended in market saturation.

Building Permits

Building permit data provide the developer with many indicators of market strength. An analysis of historical building permit trends reveals the number of units built annually, by type and location in a market area. Sharp increases or decreases in the number of residential units permitted in any year indicate market upturns or downswings. Most importantly, projections of housing unit demand can be estimated by calculating the ratio between the population and residential permit increases, and applying the ratio to population projections. Sometimes use of building permit data overestimates housing demand because of a lag between permit acquisition and unit completion. The number of certificates of occupancy issued can be used to determine if this lag is substantial enough to affect analysis results based on permits issued.

Commercial building permits can indicate the direction of demand for housing. New commercial activity creates employment, and with employment comes an increase in population. This can indicate a need for new housing.

There are two convenient sources for local and national building permit data. The Bureau of the Census publishes monthly reports of housing units authorized by building permits and public contracts. The planning or building department of any local government also keeps current and historic building permit data. In addition, many city and county planning offices can provide building permit spot maps, which allow the developer to track the direction of growth by indicating areas of active development.[7]

Absorption of Space

The absorption of space in a market is a broad indicator of market potential. Absorption "provides the framework of possibilities for each use within which the specific allocation among uses must be accomplished."[8]

The historical rate of absorption of housing units or floor area (square footage) can serve as a measurement of the potential depth of a market. High absorption rates in a market area indicate a healthy market in which the developer can probably find a niche. Low absorption rates may indicate a saturated or depressed market.

Historical absorption rates also show cycles where a building upturn produces overbuilding in a development type, which causes a decrease in building until the inventory is absorbed. Building cycles indicate market directions. A housing upturn signals population increases, which indicate potential need for new commercial and office space, and vice versa.

Developers also should carefully examine absorption rates in the planned product. High absorption may mean the market for a particular product is becoming saturated. Developers should inventory new and planned construction of the product type to gauge the remaining market.

Vacancy Rates

Vacancy rates are one of the most useful near-term market indicators for rental properties. Five percent is considered the frictional vacancy rate for housing. This rate allows for movement of households to new dwelling units without affecting the supply-and-demand equilibrium. Traditionally, a vacancy rate under five percent is considered low. Low vacancy rates may indicate that a market exists for new housing. High vacancy rates indicate overbuilding or population declines, and are a prediction of a fall in rental rates and home prices. A rising vacancy rate is an indication of potential market saturation.

Vacancy rates also can be used as a method of determining the amount of time it will take for the current housing supply to be absorbed. After allowing for a five percent frictional vacancy rate, the remaining vacancy rate can be multiplied by the total number of units absorbed per year. The resulting figure will be the projected number of years required to completely absorb the market area's rental housing inventory.

The Postal Service and local housing authorities occasionally perform surveys revealing vacancy data on the entire housing stock in a community or neighborhood.

Consumer Research

Consumer research is used to study and analyze selected groups of people. Depending on the purpose of the research, consumer groups studied can be representative of all potential consumers within a defined geographic market area, consumers from specific lifestyle or demographic groups, occupants of competitive facilities, or occupants of a specific project.

Basic qualitative facts about a market area can be learned from consumer research, including:

- Demographic characteristics within a defined market area
- Identification of target markets
- Marketability of a proposed project
- Design, size, mix and features of units
- Project amenities
- Acceptable prices or rent levels
- Market opportunities
- Image the project should convey
- Advertising and marketing strategies

In addition to the initial analysis, consumer research can be used to monitor and improve the performance of existing projects. Focus groups and random sample surveys are examples of different approaches to consumer research. In an ongoing project, buyers can be questioned about their motivations and degrees of satisfaction.

Focus Groups

A typical focus group is composed of eight to twelve persons who represent a particular market segment. The group is led by a moderator who explores topics related to home purchasing, such as:

- How people make decisions about buying homes
- How they feel about their experience
- How much space is needed
- What features are important
- Pricing

The moderator stimulates discussion and leads into pertinent topics, but does not offer opinions.

Focus groups should seek input from actual buyers of a particular product type. Focus group sessions are held in comfortable accommodations, often in a facility designed for the purpose. As an inducement to attend, refreshments are served, and gifts, cash payments, or gift certificates are distributed.

Focus group research can be used by itself, or as the first step in a more extensive research effort. It provides a highly flexible research technique, which can provide results in a short time, at a reasonable cost, with minimal logistical effort and with immediate feedback.

Random Sample Surveys

Random sample surveys can be conducted by mail, by telephone, or in person. Random sample surveys are a good approach to obtaining current information about the population within a defined market area and its preferences. Such surveys are a first step in performing a cluster analysis, which is a method of defining buyer profiles. In cluster analysis, consumers are surveyed to determine their product preferences. Consumer types with similar preferences are classified, and buyer profiles based on these preferences developed.

Each type of consumer research has its advantages. The decision regarding how to perform consumer research depends on the particular circumstances surrounding the proposed project, including the degree of perceived risk.

Feasibility

Market analysis forecasts rates of absorption and potential income streams, but the basic issue—project feasibility—depends on the long-term relationship between projected revenues and costs. In performing a feasibility study, the analyst compares revenues forecasted through market analysis with the capital and operating costs and debt service requirements anticipated by engineers, architects, managers and accountants.

Uses of a Feasibility Analysis

The feasibility analysis is a decision-making tool for the developer because it provides an estimate of the costs and benefits of building and selling a particular project. The analysis is used to determine selling prices, whether forecast absorption rates are sufficient to support development, and required financing. Feasibility analyses are often submitted with applications for project financing. Initially, however, they are generally used by the developer to make "go/no-go" decisions.

A feasibility analysis worksheet can identify opportunities to adjust the project characteristics to enhance revenues or reduce costs. If computerized, revenue and cost data can be manipulated to test project assumptions and alternative project concepts and designs. This process is called cash flow analysis and is discussed below.

Development of a Feasibility Analysis

The three major steps in the development of a feasibility analysis are:

- Determining the developer's objectives
- Determining the risks associated with the project
- Determining the financial feasibility of the project[9]

Developer's Objectives

The developer should clearly define his/her objectives for a particular project. The developer may be pursuing capital gains, hoping to achieve a large future cash flow, using the development as a hedge against inflation, or hoping to realize tax benefits.

Risk Determination

The market study will predict market changes, but other risks such as inflation, interest rate changes and the legal ramifications of rezoning and development must also be analyzed and predicted to the extent possible.

Financial Feasibility

Cash flow projections predict revenues resulting from the sale or rental of units, using market study absorption rates and unit prices. Costs are projected for the same time period. The net difference between revenues and costs is the developer's cash flow. A typical cash flow statement is shown in Figure 1.4.

Time is an important consideration when making cost and revenue predictions. A feasibility analysis forecasting several years into the future has a high margin of error.[10] Where long-term forecasts are used, estimates should be continually revised based on current information.

A feasibility study often includes several alternative courses of action (scenarios), with an analysis of the objectives, project risks and financial feasibility of each. If financial feasibility is the principal decision-making criterion, the present value of cash flow from each alternative is calculated. These present values allow the developer to make an accurate comparison of return in current dollars.

Figure 1.4 Sample Cash Flow Statement

Years	1	2	3	4	5
Revenues					
Sale of Units	$750,000	$1,050,000	$1,200,000	$1,500,000	$750,000
Total Revenues	750,000	1,050,000	1,200,000	1,500,000	750,000
Costs					
Land Acquisition	225,000	0	0	0	0
Development Costs					
Planning	22,500	31,500	36,000	45,000	22,500
Site improvements	22,500	31,500	36,000	45,000	22,500
Engineering	18,750	26,250	30,000	37,500	18,750
Architecture	18,750	26,250	30,000	37,500	18,750
Construction	337,500	472,500	540,000	675,000	337,500
Administrative Costs	7,500	10,500	12,000	15,000	7,500
Financing	30,000	42,000	48,000	60,000	30,000
Total Costs	682,500	640,500	732,000	915,000	457,500
Total Cash Flow	**$ 67,500**	**$409,500**	**$468,000**	**$585,000**	**$292,500**

Summary

Every project starts with a market analysis. Some are intuitive, seat-of-the-pants guesses about the market. Others are merely a response to the market analysis of another developer/builder. But the more accurate the analysis, the more likely the project is to succeed, and at the lowest possible risk.

Professional market analysis is important to the developer because real estate markets are constantly changing and evolving. Today's consumer is more sophisticated than ever before, and new approaches to analysis are necessary to accurately gauge the market. The developer must define the market area, know the competition and evaluate market indicators. Consumer research can be undertaken to identify target markets and buyer preferences. The services of professional market consulting firms are cost-effective because they contribute to the design of an efficient and marketable product.

Based on market analysis, preliminary project plans can be developed (Figure 1.5) and a feasibility analysis can be conducted. The feasibility analysis aids the developer in making "go/no-go" choices. The market and feasibility analyses help determine criteria for site selection. Chapter Two discusses site selection criteria and techniques in detail.

Information Sources
U.S. Government

U.S. Department of Commerce Bureau of Census, Washington, D.C.

The Commerce Department's Census Bureau publishes a variety of documents containing demographic and business data. A selected list of publications follows:

- *Bureau of the Census Catalogue* is updated periodically and provides information about all publications issued by the Bureau of the Census.
- *Series P-25 and P-26* provide updated population estimates and projections at the state, county and town levels. Includes per capita income estimates.
- The *Annual Housing Survey*, published in two series. The first is a survey of housing characteristics providing general and regionally specific information on the United States. The second provides similar information in greater detail, categorized by SMSA.
- *Housing Authorized by Building Permits and Public Contracts* (Series C-40). Monthly data categorized by state MSA and individual towns, grouped by county.
- *Census of Retail Trade*, published in five-year intervals, contains detailed sales statistics to the county level.

U.S. Department of Commerce, Bureau of Economic Analysis, Washington, D.C.

- *County and City Data Book,* published annually by U.S. Department of Commerce Bureau of Economic Analysis, Washington, D.C.
- *Survey of Current Business*, published monthly by the Bureau of Economic Analysis, contains detailed business statistics including employment, commodity prices, finances, industrial product sales, consumer expenditure data, and income figures for states, counties and metropolitan areas.

U.S. Department of Labor, Bureau of Labor Statistics, Washington, D.C.

The Bureau of Labor Statistics publishes periodical data on employment and earnings, consumer price movements and current labor force and unemployment statistics in *Consumer Expenditures and Income.*

State Government

Bureaus of Employment keep monthly tabulations on total employment and unemployment at the state as well as local levels.

Local Government

School District Administrations
School enrollments are a source of data.

Vehicle Registration Bureaus
Population trends can be discerned from annual changes in registrations.

Planning Commissions
These agencies are a good source for local building activity statistics.

Figure 1.5 Concept master plan

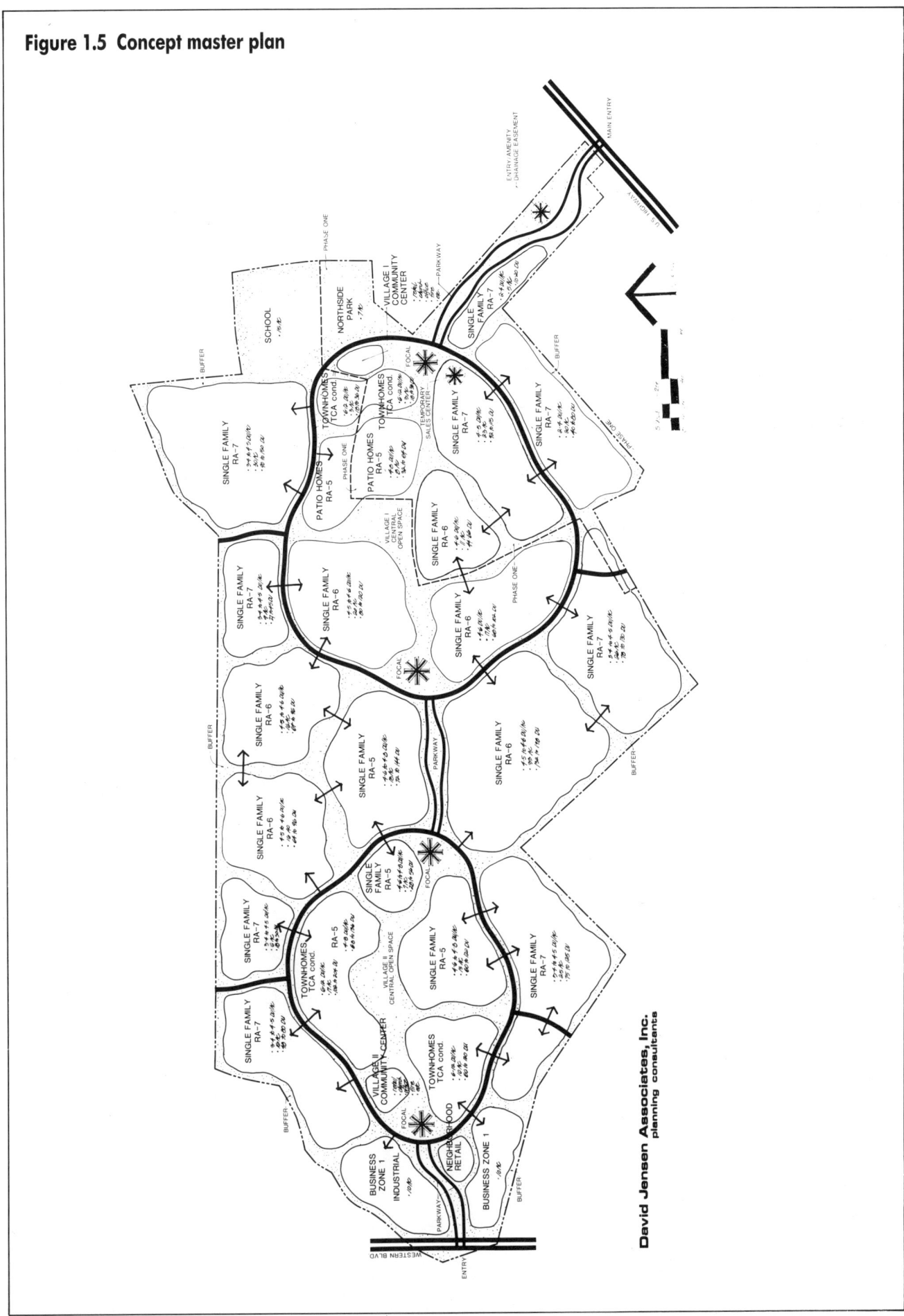

Local Chambers of Commerce

These organizations often can provide local information on population, local municipalities, demographic data, housing, industry, tourism activity and transportation.

Industry Organizations

Trends within various industries can be tracked by reading publications from local or national industry organizations.

Private Publications

A variety of publications are available to assist in market analysis. A selected list of widely used publications follows:

- *Sales and Marketing Management*, published by Bill Communications, Inc., New York, is a monthly publication. It contains statistical compilations, including "Survey of Buying Power," which give current estimates of U.S. and Canadian geographic variations in population, income and retail trade.
- *The Dollars and Cents of Shopping Centers* has been published every three years since 1960 by the Urban Land Institute, Washington, D.C. The study is a principal source of comparative data on the income and expenses of shopping center operations.
- *The Office Network*, Houston, Texas, publishes an annual survey of office-related statistics for selected municipalities across the country.
- *Black's Guide,* Redbank, N. J., provides detailed surveys of office space conditions for various regions throughout the U.S.
- *Community Builders Handbook Series* by Urban Land Institute, Washington, D.C., is a continually updated series of land development reference sources.
- *Dodge Construction Reports* by McGraw-Hill, Inc., New York, provides statistics on construction activity. Data are available for each state down to county level of detail.

Research Departments of Local Banks

Bank deposits can provide information on local population and economic trends. Bank officers also can supply insights helpful in evaluating project feasibility.

Newspapers

Newspaper circulation quantities provide information on population trends. Some newspapers have their own research departments, which collect updated information on local area economics and demographics.

Utility and Telephone Companies

These companies are a source of current population estimates for their service areas. They often perform their own forecasts, which, if obtainable, are useful in market-related population projections.

Footnotes

1. "40% of U.S. Households Have Broken Traditional Mold," *Multi-Housing News*, June, 1984, pp. 24-25.

2. Consumer Price Index for the United States, Bureau of Labor Statistics, Washington, D.C. 1985 (change was from 217.4 to 322.2).

3. Bivins, Jacquelin, "Developers Track the Data," *Chain Store Executive*, March, 1984, pp. 80-83; and George L. Tresnack and Frederick Flick, "Two Trends for Thought," *Real Estate Today*, September 1984, pp. 11-16.

4. David Jensen Associates, Inc., *Community Design Guidelines, Responding to a Changing Market*, National Association of Home Builders, 1984, p. 10.

5. Roulac, Stephen, "Planning, Financing and Developing Pioneering Projects," *Urban Land*, Oct., 1984, p. F-11.

6. Tiebout, Charles M., *The Community Economic Base Study*, New York Commission for Economic Development, Dec. 1962, Supplemental Paper No. 16.

7. Urban Land Institute, *Residential Development Handbook*, Washington, D.C. 1982, p. 25.

8. Wilburn, Michael D., and Gladstone, Robert M., "Optimizing Development Profits in Large Scale Real Estate Projects," *Technical Bulletin No. 67*, Urban Land Institute, Washington, D.C., 1972, p. 18.

9. Barrett, G. Vincent, and and Blair, John P., *How to Conduct and Analyze Real Estate Market and Feasibility Studies*, Van Nostrand Reinhold Company, Inc., New York, 1982, pp. 64-66.

10. *Residential Development Handbook*, Urban Land Institute, Washington, D.C., 1982, p. 91.

Chapter Two

Finding the Land

This chapter will show you how to shop for land for development. But first, two warnings:

- Define what you are looking for—for example, a site for apartments, or single-family homes, or townhouses. You must have a target to know if you have hit it.
- Second, don't speculate when you buy land. It is foolish to buy land with no specific use in mind. There are enough unavoidable risks in the real estate development business without assuming the additional risk that the price of undeveloped land will appreciate faster than interest rates. During periods of high interest rates, a developer is fortunate if the value of the land keeps pace with accumulating interest charges.

This chapter assumes that you know the type of product you will be building, and that you are looking for land for residential development. Searches for commercial, industrial and office land will not be covered. Many of the techniques suggested for finding residential land can of course be used for finding nonresidential land parcels.

The premise of this chapter is that you are unfamiliar with the community where you plan to build. This may be the case if you are looking for land outside your community, if you are just entering the real estate industry, or if your community is large, with submarkets.

If you are looking for land in the community in which you live and that community is relatively small, you will probably already know the desirable residential neighborhoods and the location of the employment centers. And you will probably have contacts in the industry who may help you.

Imagine yourself two miles above a community looking down, with an overview of the entire area. The decision-making process for selecting land involves three steps. First, the overall community is reviewed. Second, the area or neighborhood with the greatest development potential is identified. Third, the optimal location within the neighborhood for your proposed project is selected. This chapter will help you obtain the information you need to make well-founded decisions about the community and the neighborhood. Chapter Three covers the details of site analysis and selection.

Community Analysis

Much of the basic information required for community analysis is derived through the market analysis process described in Chapter One. Employment, income, and other demographic data help answer the key question: "Is there a need in the community for the type of project I want to do?" As you move forward in the land selection process, you can use the following sources of information and input to help you reach an informed decision.

Appraisers

All proposed projects eventually must go through the appraisal process because lenders do not make real estate loans without appraisals. Appraisers also can help with your information needs. In analyzing whether a community can absorb your project, you need to know if you can be competitive, and if you are building directly into an overbuilt market. You need to know if competing projects will be under construction at the same time. You need to know prevailing market conditions, such as rents, sales prices, capitalization rates, and expense ratios.

Find the best appraisal firm in town. This is easily accomplished by interviewing mortgage bankers. Their knowledge of appraisers is excellent. Be sure to request referrals to an appraiser who has expertise in the area of real estate in which you are considering a project. The excellent industrial appraiser probably will not be right for a residential project.

Once you have a name or two, set up an appointment to talk to the appraisers about your project and determine whether they have the information you want, and how you can work together. Most appraisers will do a complete study of the market for you, including surveying the other appraisers in the community regarding any knowledge that they might possess about the market. Some appraisers also will do out-of-town market research, although their knowledge of out-of-town markets would be more limited.

Some large local appraisal firms and private publishers publish periodic real estate market reports. These publications typically cover all new projects in the planning or permit stage, all conveyances of title, all new home permits, and a gossip page for market information that cannot be documented—a "heard on the street" column.

Newspapers

If you can, subscribe to and read the local newspaper for at least six months before you decide to proceed with a planned project. Pay particular attention to three sections of the paper: the classified advertisements, the business pages, and the community news section.

The classified advertisements will reveal an overbuilt condition as fast as any other source. It takes no particular genius to decipher, "First month rent free if you sign a six-month lease," or, "Your choice of a free swimming pool, European vacation, or new BMW if you buy one of our new patio home villas this weekend." These ads communicate desperation to sell a slow-moving product.

"Classifieds" also provide information on competing products in the market and their location. Use a road map and mark each project's location with a code as you read the "classifieds." Keep a separate notebook to write down the code number, with pertinent information about the project. Such additional information might include the prices or rents; giveaways, if any; the type of product (e.g., single-family, townhouses, amenities); and hours models are open. This road map will be referred to later during the search for a suitable neighborhood and individual parcel.

The business and community news sections of the newspaper provide information on plant closings, new industries in the community, problems with city hall, law suits against developments and developers, school problems, crime problems, articles on possible overbuilding, information on proposed rent controls or building or utility hook-up moratoriums, and articles announcing new real estate developments such as office buildings and apartments. In short, reading these sections of the newspaper provides you with a basic feel for the community and its problems and opportunities. This resource is of particular value if you are located outside of the community you wish to study. If you are so busy you would have difficulty reading another newspaper (or don't even read your own community's), then you may want to subscribe to a clipping service to provide only those articles that are pertinent.

Economic Surveys

Many consulting firms provide economic information about a particular community. Commercial brokers such as Coldwell/Banker publish research reports from time to time. Firms that advertise "market analysis" in their description of services can be commissioned for specialized studies. Such firms include David Jensen Associates in Denver, The Goodkin Group in La Jolla, CA, and Robert Siegel & Associates and Hebert/Smolkin Associates, both in New Orleans. Others, such as Robert Fuller Associates in Denver, produce economic surveys at regular intervals and sell them to the general public. While not specifically geared to your needs, general reports can provide good market information at a relatively low cost.

Request economic information from the local chamber of commerce. Join the local home builders association and/or multihousing association to obtain statistical data on building permits and vacancy levels. Plot building permits over the past ten years and compare with employment. Is there a correlation? If so, what are current employment growth forecasts? Analyze building permits. Is there an identifiable cycle? Are you about to buy as the cycle turns down?

Windshield Survey

Finally, nothing replaces getting in your car and driving through the community you are studying. If you are thinking of building new homes in an area, pay particular attention to "for sale" signs. Too many indicate a problem—too few may indicate a market need.

Talk to the sales people in model home complexes. Ask them how sales are, who their strongest competition is, what customers are demanding. The accuracy of information obtained from such obviously biased sources is questioned by some, talking to the competition can be very helpful and informative.

If your interest is in apartments, observe "for lease" signs—both the number and size. When half the building is covered with a "now renting" sign you know that there is a problem. Talk to the leasing agents. Are there waiting lists?

Drive through subdivisions to see how many houses are under construction. Try to estimate the rate of absorption by counting the completed and under-construction houses, and dividing by the number of months that the sales office has been open (ask the sales person).

Dodge Reports

Construction activity is reported in most cities by daily *Dodge Reports*. There may be similar reports published by others in the community in which you are interested. This report shows all permits by address, contractor, owner, and permit value. If you have these plotted over a period of several months, you will have an excellent indication of where construction activity is centered, and what product is selling the best in that market.

Real Estate Agents

If you are in the business of selling new homes, talking to real estate agents involved in residential sales can be invaluable. Agents are responsible for a large and growing proportion of total new home sales. Approximately 40 percent of the new homes in this writer's community are made by real estate agents.

Ask successful high-volume agents what features they think are important to your project's success. Ask their opinions regarding prime locations. Their continual review of the product that is available, and their attempts to satisfy their clients' needs place them in an extraordinarily good position to provide you with valuable information.

Neighborhood Analysis

Let's assume that you decide to develop your proposed project in the community you have studied. The proposed project will not face adverse competition, and in your opinion will receive acceptance in the marketplace.

The next step is to determine the area of the community in which to locate your project. Do not make the mistake of considering appropriate zoning as the only criterion. The three most important success factors in real estate are still "location, location, and location." Appropriately zoned land is often in an undesirable location.

Similarly, don't let price become your sole criterion. Often an infill project can be quite appealing. If you decide to do infill, be prepared to jump through regulatory and political hoops. Most communities say that they support infill, but when the going gets tough, you may find they are no longer behind you. Neighborhood groups are almost certain to oppose infill proposals. No doubt, those neighbors have used that vacant land as a playground for several years and are not about to lose it without a fight. If the density of the planned project is higher than the existing density, expect an even tougher fight. You will have to counter allegations that higher densities will create crime, increase congestion and air pollution, overcrowd the schools, and so on.

Where do you begin to look? Don't be a pioneer, particularly when you're new to town. Go where the action is. Find the other builders and developers and assume that they made rational decisions. Above all else, you need the sales traffic that is generated when development activity is centered in one geographic area. Nothing is as lonely as having a project off by itself with no traffic. People like to shop and their time is limited. They like to go to one location, do all their shopping, and make a decision. If you are too far away, they may not have the energy or the time to go out of their way to find you. Regional shopping centers and, more recently, auto dealer parks are thriving on this principle.

How do you find the action?

Catalogues and Magazines

Retrieve the road map mentioned in the section on classified newspaper advertising above to provide information on the location of new or competing products. Because builders and developers choose different media for advertising, it is important to examine several different publications. Many communities with brisk new construction activity are served by four-color magazines that list all of a builder's projects, complete with maps. Use the magazines and other advertising information to provide additional locations on your road map and list project information in a separate notebook.

If apartments are your area of interest, find existing complexes by perusing the yellow pages or apartment-finding guides. Again, mark them on your map.

When analyzing the information on the road map, remember that your product must be consistent with its surroundings. You can't build luxury homes in a neighborhood of apartment buildings. If you have a confusing array of projects on your map, remove those that are inconsistent with your proposed project.

Where are the clusters of similar products? These clusters broadly define the area in which you need to concentrate your search as you get closer to the final purchase decision.

Now the target neighborhood must be investigated and scrutinized. Even though it is a much smaller geographic area than the entire community, the job of analyzing the neighborhood is in some respects even more complex.

Get back in your car to investigate why some projects within the target neighborhood are more successful than others. The increased market information that you now possess will allow you to understand more than when you first drove through the community to conduct the "windshield survey."

Make sure that you take your road map and supporting notes to designate which of the projects are successful. See if there is a geographic pattern, or some other relationship among the successful projects within the already defined market area. For example, are all the successful projects near a lake or other water feature? Are they relatively close-in? Are they near an undeveloped nature area? School district boundaries are often a dividing line between successful and unsuccessful projects.

Aerial Photographs

If you don't already have one, get a telephone directory of the community you are studying. Look up "Photographers—Commercial" or "Photographers—Aerial." Ask if recent photographs of the area you are studying are available. Existing photographs are less expensive and quicker to obtain than specially commissioned ones. Explain your needs to the photographer. Your road map will indicate the rough boundaries of the area you want photographed. The photographer can suggest altitudes for taking the photographs. An aerial photograph will have less resolution as the camera goes higher, but the photograph will not show the relationships you want to examine if it is taken too close to the ground (Figure 2.1).

Lay the aerial photograph and the road map side-by-side. Identify the product you have determined is comparable to yours on the aerial map. Locate and identify major streets, rivers, canals, railroad tracks, natural boundaries, airports, retail centers, hospitals, schools, public transportation routes, any major employment in the vicinity, and bridges. Note if there appear to be grading or clearing activities. Obtain a traffic map and note how much traffic the major streets carry. Analyze the pattern of these physical features and the pattern of successful and unsuccessful projects. Are there relationships?

You may wish at this point to drive the area again to identify any objects in the aerial photo that are unknown to you. Remember that not all projects are unsuccessful because of poor location—some are poorly designed, have ineffective marketing, or need new management. In any case, the purpose of this step is to determine if there are physical reasons for a project's failure. If you find something obvious, such as that all the projects in the airport's flight path are having problems, you definitely can rule out the flight path area.

Helicopter

Many developers believe that nothing provides a faster and more complete education than viewing a site and its surroundings from a helicopter. The helicopter offers some of the same advantages as an aerial photograph in showing the relationships of a parcel to its surroundings. But the helicopter offers the opportunity to really see the parcel:

Figure 2.1 Aerial photograph of site vicinity

David Jensen Associates, Inc.

if you're too high you can fly lower. An aerial photograph may be current, but the helicopter ride is even more immediate. The pilot may have taken other builders on similar rides and may be willing to provide additional information.

A couple of tips: Plan your itinerary. Make sure the pilot knows what you want to see and the sequence in which you want to see it. Take along a camera. If it is a still camera, mark your map (the one on which you planned the flight path) when you take the picture, including the direction from which the picture was taken. This way you can identify your pictures when they are developed. You may also wish to use a video camera, which enables you to review your entire flight at a later date.

Site Location

By now you have identified the neighborhoods or belts within neighborhoods where you want to locate your proposed project. The method of locating individual parcels for consideration will depend on the type of property you are seeking.

Existing Single-Family Lots

If your objective is to purchase finished lots from a developer, you may be able to buy lots in an existing subdivision. Most likely, you will identify existing subdivisions during your fly-overs, or from the aerial photographs. If there is any development activity within the subdivision, a few questions normally will provide you with information about the developer. If there is no current activity, you can obtain the name of the development and the developer by visiting the map room at local county offices and reading the names from the recorded plat.

On the other hand, you may find that the development is already sold out, the price of the lots is too high, or the location is good but not quite what you wanted. In that case you may want to determine if any new subdivisions will be available soon. The first steps are to read your appraisal report again (if you have one), or to ask your appraiser to prepare a list of proposed new subdivisions. Several other sources can also be used here. Savings and loan corporation personnel are usually well-informed and helpful. Real estate bankers, the local home builders association, engineering firms, city planning officials, and the records of planning and zoning boards are other good sources of information.

Undeveloped Parcels

You need to decide whether you are going to use the services of a real estate broker before you proceed with exploring the vacant land parcels in your predetermined area. If you ask for a broker's help, and then find a parcel on your own, you may end up with a dispute over whether a commission is due. You may not need a broker until you are ready to examine and compare alternative sites with the one you already have located.

Assume for the moment that a broker is not needed. (The subject of broker services will be explored later in this chapter.) Let us proceed with how to locate vacant parcels within predefined boundaries.

First, obtain any zoning maps that are available from the local zoning authority. If any comprehensive planning has been undertaken, the city planning department should be able to provide maps that show the results of that planning. You will need either a new city road map or the city zoning map. The bigger the scale the better. The zoning maps are particularly good because they show the individual platted parcels, as well as the applicable zoning, and are usually quite a bit larger than a road map. Making copies of pages of a "zone atlas" and taping their match lines together will provide you with a map that shows the area you're interested in, and is easy to use. Zoning maps provide a good perspective on the shape and size of a parcel without having a survey.

With the map in hand, it's time to get in the car again. Drive the entire area (and that means every street), and mark the map with all vacant parcels that appear to have both the appropriate zoning for your development and the size you are after. Generally, it is easiest if the property is already zoned single-family, but agricultural zoning also should be considered. Note any signs showing the property is for sale. Don't ignore a parcel just because it is not posted for sale. In theory, all private land is for sale at the right price.

Where the land is posted for sale, you can call to obtain information on price, terms, availability of surveys (including topographical), utility availability, building or use restrictions, or any problems or costs known to the seller that would either prevent, make difficult, or present an unusual cost for your proposed development. There will be more discussion of these issues in Chapter Three when the topic of site feasibility analysis is covered.

Chances are you will not see a sign on many of the parcels. Ownership maps are sometimes available through the county clerk's office. If your area has title companies, their title "plants" are invaluable for determining the ownership of a particular parcel. Information from such a "plant" is always more current than an ownership map, and much easier to use. Once you have determined the ownership, you need to pick up the telephone and talk to the owner, or, better yet, make an appointment for a face-to-face meeting. Letters may be easy for you to write, but they are also easy for a potential seller to dismiss.

Multifamily Parcels

Identifying the owners of multifamily parcels is similar to the process described in the preceding section on undeveloped single-family parcels. Because obtaining multifamily rezoning is so difficult in most communities, it is much easier if you can find a parcel that is already appropriately zoned. If you cannot find a parcel zoned for multifamily use, there is always the possibility of obtaining a rezoning of either an agricultural parcel or a single-family parcel. Be cautious, however; the rezoning process will be long and difficult.

It is axiomatic that any existing neighborhood groups will oppose rezoning. Not only will these groups testify in opposition at local zoning board hearings; they are increasingly likely to file suits in district courts to reverse favorable rulings by local authorities. You may find the piece of land is zoned commercial or office, and because of its location reflects a value indicative of apartment use. If you can build on the parcel without a hearing, you're in luck. But if a public hearing is needed—beware! Owners of single-family homes tend to vehemently oppose multifamily development even though they often have been apartment dwellers themselves in the past, and may have children or parents living in apartments now.

The point is not to overlook commercial- or office-zoned parcels as potential multifamily sites. It is usually easier to downgrade zoning from commercial or office to apartment, than to upgrade zoning, as is the case going from agricultural or single-family to apartment. But don't be deceived; neighborhood groups will oppose even a downgrade in zoning if it's to apartment use.

Broker Services

While real estate broker services can be expensive, they can expose you to a broader market than you might otherwise reach. Commissions range from five to ten percent of the parcel purchase price. If you have a license to sell real estate and are completely familiar with your community, you may want to earn the commission yourself or to negotiate a lower price with the seller, with the understanding that no "selling office" commission will be paid. Note that some sellers object to this arrangement.

If you find yourself buried under your current workload and wonder how you can ever find the time to locate the next parcel of ground to keep your company moving ahead, you probably need to consider a broker's services. Your time and talent may be better spent working on problems with which you are extremely familiar, making it profitable to turn over the search for land to a broker.

All brokers are not created equal. Finding the right broker may be as difficult as finding the right parcel of land. In many communities, there are brokers who specialize in the acquisition of land for builders and developers. Ask for recommendations. Sources of recommendation include some of the people to whom you have already spoken. The real estate attorney you use in your home community should be able to recommend a real estate attorney in the community you are considering. That new attorney, in turn, would be in a good position to recommend any local real estate brokers. If you are working with an appraiser, he/she can also provide you with brokers' names. Title companies, lending departments of financial institutions, and your local home builders association also can provide recommendations.

Review the notes you took when you were driving the neighborhood searching for signs. You may find that one or two brokers dominate the listings. This dominance indicates detailed knowledge of the real estate market in the neighborhood. If a dominant broker has been recommended by other sources, he/she may be able to provide the service you need; in any case, if you find the same name coming up from several sources, you have a good endorsement.

Brokers are used frequently by investors desiring anonymity. "Dummy" corporations or partnerships often are created with brokers acting as their agents, so no one but the brokers know the purchaser's identity. This device is used to prevent a holdout seller from raising a price drastically because he/she realizes the purchasers want to put together a large block of land. Other builder/developer companies are concerned that a seller will charge a higher price if the seller knows who the purchaser is. Prices have a tendency to increase when a large, publicly held company becomes interested in a parcel of land.

Chapter Three will discuss pricing. You should not purchase a parcel of land at a price that makes you noncompetitive with surrounding products. If you use a real estate broker, he/she should provide you with prices for comparable sites in the area. The broker typically will have more information regarding the terms of the sales that have occurred than the appraiser. Without knowledge of the terms of the sale, you cannot analyze the basic cost of the land.

In summary, the arguments for using a real estate broker to work with you on the purchase of a land parcel are as follows:

- The qualified broker has a level of knowledge concerning the local real estate market that you will not acquire within the context of a single land purchase.
- The broker will free your time to work on problems that only you can solve, or problems to which your knowledge is better applied.
- The broker will allow you to remain anonymous.
- The broker will serve as a middleman if you prefer to distance yourself from the negotiations.

One word of caution. The broker can make a living only if he/she earns a commission. Some sellers do not want to pay commissions to real estate brokers. Most brokers will not show you a parcel of land if they cannot collect a commission. Consequently, if you rely on a real estate broker you may not see all available parcels.

Ask the broker to explain the status of each vacant land parcel indicated on the maps you have created. If you choose to pursue a parcel on which the seller will pay no commission, you can negotiate a compensation agreement with your broker. This agreement ensures that he/she will continue to help with the purchase of the parcel after the purchase agreement is signed, and increases the likelihood that he/she will want to work with you in the future.

The issue of how much you will pay a broker in such a circumstance will vary based on the amount of effort expended by the broker, his/her role in the negotiations, and the greed of the seller. One approach is to make the seller an offer based on comparables. Since the seller does not have to pay a commission, deduct one-half (the seller's half) of a normal commission from the sales price. You, in effect, agree to split the savings with the seller. The amount deducted could then be paid to your broker.

Miscellaneous Sources

No one's knowledge of an area is perfect, complete, and continually current. You must remain forever vigilant to the possibility of previously unconsidered sites becoming available. You should continue to survey both local newspapers and the Friday edition of the *Wall Street Journal*.

Other builders can be another source of information about developed or undeveloped parcels. Builders often misjudge inventory needs by being too optimistic regarding absorption rates. They will cut back on their inventory by selling off land to other builders. If you see a parcel that has been owned for some time and shows no evidence of development, consider calling the other builder.

Other businesses—such as utilities, railroads, oil companies, and insurance companies—often purchase land for a proposed use that never comes to fruition. Don't be put off if you find that a major corporation owns a piece of real estate. You may find them very anxious to sell, and sometimes at bargain prices. Banks and savings and loans often acquire real estate through foreclosure. Many times, the site is excellent, but the developer wasn't. The advantage of buying real estate from a financial institution is that they generally offer a ready source of financing.

City and town governments also may have desirable land parcels for sale. Municipalities normally acquire large tracts for parks and recreation, schools, fire and police stations, and municipal offices, which may not be built, or may not use all the land purchased for them.

Summary

The purpose of this chapter has been to provide the reader with techniques for researching the community, the neighborhood, and alternative sites. An extensive amount of research has been suggested. If conducted well, this investigation should greatly reduce the risks of failure due to an improperly located project. There is nothing mysterious about finding good land. A huge amount of raw data must be accumulated, processed, and evaluated. The evaluation process should be rational, but also creative and intuitive. Because land development potential is subjective, two individuals with the same information are likely to reach different conclusions.

In the end, selecting among alternative sites is often a matter of "gut" feel. Don't allow yourself to freeze over that decision. At the same time, if you're frustrated in attempts to find parcels, don't rationalize the selection of a bad location because it is available. Chapter Three gives criteria for final site selection.

Chapter Three

Raw Land Analysis and Site Selection

Once suitable sites have been located, the focus narrows. Each site must be analyzed to determine whether it can be developed profitably, and must be compared to every other site to determine which site offers the greatest profit potential. Good location does not mean that a site should be purchased at any price. Other important factors include the condition of the land; offsite features (water, sewer, utilities) that need to be installed and paid for, and their availability; any easement or title problems; and whether the land is appropriately zoned.

Another NAHB publication, *Land Buying Checklist*, serves as a workbook for developers who are evaluating land for purchase. This 36-page checklist by southern California builder Ralph M. Lewis enables the builder to examine all critical factors—physical, legal, financial, governmental—necessary for confident land purchase decisions and avoidance of costly mistakes.

Site Factors

Each parcel of land you are considering has a different set of site factors. These site factors influence the price that you finally pay for the raw land. The term "site factors" as used here includes the following: transportation, utilities (gas, electricity, telephone), sewer and water, size and shape of parcel, topography, soils, easements and encroachments, and deed restrictions (Figure 3.1). The cost of the raw land may be the beginning point in determining the ultimate profitability of the project, but the costs associated with site factors also must be calculated and added to the cost of the raw land. In this manner a comparison between sites can be made. For example, a 15-acre parcel at $750,000 with no offsite costs is less expensive than a 15-acre parcel with raw land costs of $400,000, but with an additional $400,000 in costs for extending roads, sewer, and water to the site.

Your fact-finding should include discussions with the local planning office. For example, the planner may state that 2,000 feet of roadway must be constructed at your expense before approval is granted for your project. To estimate the cost of building that roadway, or many of the other required site development costs, obtain the help of a reputable civil engineering firm. The civil engineering firm will be familiar with local development costs because of their experience in negotiating and estimating subdivision improvements and infrastructure contracts.

Transportation

Does your site have any ingress or egress problems? Will it be necessary to pay for road improvements to bring paved roads to the site? If paved roads are needed to bring traffic to your site, who is going to pay for them—you or the local county or municipality? Is the site landlocked? If so, can an easement be obtained to bring a road across someone else's property without a legal battle? What will the easement cost you? If an easement is necessary, who will maintain the road after the project is completed? Will there be a need to modify existing public roads to provide median cuts in appropriate places? These median cuts should line up with streets within your project, allowing both right and left turns from the public roadway exterior to your site. Discussions with the agency that has jurisdiction over future roads is necessary. Traffic engineering departments may be a good place to start.

If your project will be sold to commuters, how close is freeway access or a station for commuter trains or buses? Will the subject site be at a disadvantage to other sites with respect to these commuter facilities?

Figure 3.1 Site factors

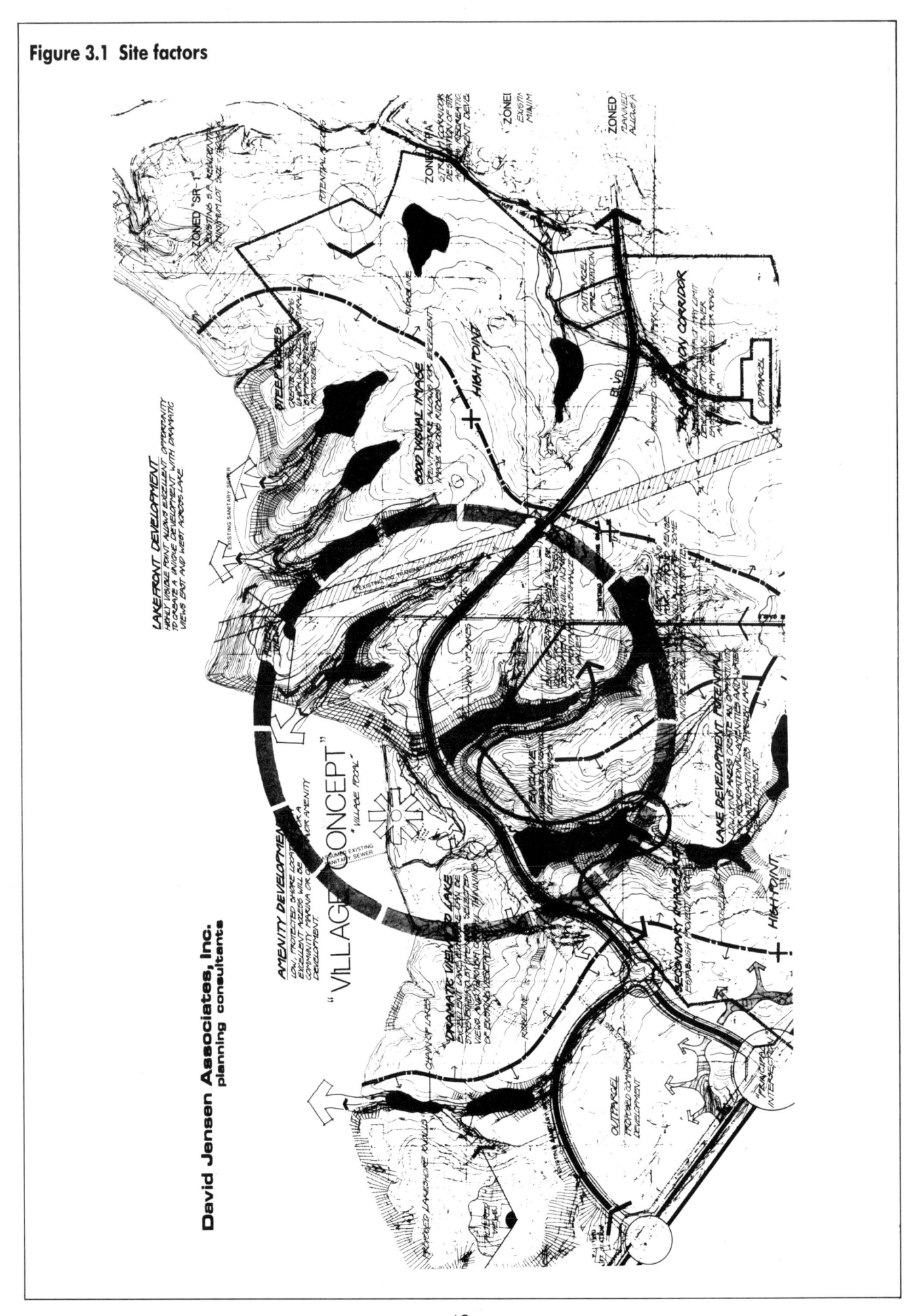

Utilities

What is the status of gas and electric utilities? The utility company may refund the cost of extending gas and electric lines both to and within your property. In almost all cases, you will have to expend the cash first, and the utility company will rebate all or a portion of those expenditures to you. The portion of expended costs rebated to you often is based on the estimated utility usage of the residences anticipated in your project. The rebate is prorated based on the proportion of installed meters to the total number of potential meters in that location.

Estimating costs for utilities involves determining not only the cost for extending those utilities, but also the carrying costs on the amounts expended to extend the utilities, and the carrying cost on the land during the time the utilities are being extended to your site. The amount of time the utility company takes to extend utilities to the site will probably be out of your control. Consequently, you must have discussions with the utility company prior to purchasing the land to ascertain a typical installation schedule.

Although telephones are not essential to the issue of whether a house is habitable, lack of telephone service can negatively impact your sales effort. Make sure that the telephone company has enough capacity in its switching stations to handle a new project. If you can, persuade the telephone company to issue a written commitment to provide service to your project by a given date.

Sewer and Water

Questions similar to those asked for gas and electricity should be asked about sewer and water. If sewer and water are being provided by a community system, how far are the nearest lines from the site, and are the lines adequate to handle the demands of the project you are considering? Expect the sewer and water lines to run in totally different directions on your site. Each must be addressed individually.

With regard to the sewer—will any extra expense be required for a pumping station? Before closing on the purchase, you will want to obtain a letter from the municipal authorities stating the availability of water and sewer services to the parcels you are considering. Make sure your purchase agreement is contingent on obtaining a satisfactory availability letter.

If the cost for extending sewer and water is prohibitively high, or if the extension of existing lines is not possible, you will need to decide whether to provide individual wells and septic tanks, or a private water and sewer system to be owned by the homeowners. The pollution of groundwater by septic tanks is becoming a major issue across the country. In New Jersey, for example, some areas require a minimum lot size of over thirty acres if a septic tank is installed. Such measures effectively preclude using septic tanks in all but the most rural areas.

Check with local authorities if you are contemplating wells and septic systems to learn what types of systems are allowable. The cost of providing a privately owned system—including the lost value of land needed for system facilities—must be analyzed carefully. In the worst case, you may find that water rights are not available to individual users or to a privately owned water and sewer company. If you cannot get water and sewer to each residence, forget the site.

It is not unusual to find that the municipality will not make a commitment regarding when they will extend utilities, and at the same time will not allow you to develop your own system. Without water and sewer, you will not be able to obtain a building permit, and thus might have to hold the land for a long time before water and sewer become available. Having to carry a large vacant land parcel for an indefinite time period due to a lack of utilities, sewer, or water is an enormous financial risk.

Also ask about water zones. Water supply normally is zoned to keep water pressure within a given range. Find out if your site has more than one water zone to contend with. If it does, each zone will have different problems. Each may come from a different direction, with resulting differences in availability.

Size and Shape of Parcel

The size of a parcel is important to you from two standpoints. The first is whether the site is too small and the second is whether the site is too big.

For example, assume that market analysis has shown that your proposed product will be absorbed at the rate of four dwelling units per month. If the parcel under consideration is three acres, and the density is to be three units per acre, it will take approximately two months to sell out the parcel. You would be finished soon after you started. It is not an economical use of your time and energy to spend six months to a year putting together a parcel that will provide you with only a two-month product supply.

Using the same set of assumptions but varying the size of the land to one hundred acres, you would now have a supply of lots that would last more than six years. You probably don't need more than a two- to three-year supply of land at any time. Having an excessive amount of land in reserve is, in effect, purchasing land on speculation. The cost of carrying an excessive land inventory increases the operating and financial risks of your business, and should be avoided.

The shape of the property affects the lot yield. The analysis used below to determine the price that can be paid for a site starts with the retail value of the project. In single-family developments, retail value is the product of multiplying the number of lots that the site yields by their retail value. Generally, the lower the lot yield, the higher the cost of site improvements per lot. Oddly shaped parcels need more roadways to reach fewer lots. The results: higher development costs and lower retail value.

It may be useful to obtain a copy of the plat or site survey and rough in the streets and lot sizes you want. This procedure usually reveals any obvious yield problems, and may quickly exclude a parcel from consideration. For example, your cursorial site plan may reveal narrow sections where lots are available along just one side of the street. In such a situation the ratio of development cost to lot value would almost double.

An example of inefficient yield from a land parcel is shown in Figure 3.2. This oddly shaped parcel was offered to builders at the same price per acre as other surrounding parcels that were not so unusual.

The lots numbered 2 and 3 in Figure 3.2 illustrate the problems presented by narrow parcels. These lots are so shallow that only a custom design would fit. The marketability of the lots is limited and the costs are high. Both the amount of street frontage and the land area within the lot add development costs substantially in excess of those a conventional lot would require. Lot 1 is extremely narrow and deep, although the land area and cost are high. Lot 4 is bizarre: the long finger of land extending from its rear boundary would add to your purchase price but would contribute little selling value.

The acreage cost of this parcel is comparable to surrounding parcels. Because of this parcel's configuration, however, the number of lots per acre (yield) will be less than the yield on surrounding parcels. If this decrease in yield is not offset by an increased value in the resulting lots, you will be operating at a cost disadvantage compared to neighboring builders. The lots discussed above and shown in Figure 3.2 do not appear to add extra value. Therefore, the price-per-acre of this parcel must be lower to reflect its inefficient configuration. The price-per-acre should drop until the cost-per-lot of the raw land on this parcel equals the cost-per-lot on the surrounding parcels.

Topography

The surface contours of the site you are considering can affect both costs and yields. A nice flat site may require little earthwork, but the same topography increases the cost of installing sewer lines. On the other hand, a sloping site will keep sewer installation costs low, but require extensive earthwork to create flat building sites. Earthwork costs increase as the slope of the site increases, and can reach a point where the preparation cost exceeds the value of the site. When a lot's improvement cost (including earthwork) exceeds its retail value, the lot will not be developed and the yield on the total parcel will diminish. In steeply sloped terrains, existing water pressure zones may not be adequate to serve all of the site. In this case, it may not be cost-effective to develop the few lots outside the existing zones.

Site topography also affects drainage costs. Obtain a flood hazard map prepared by the U.S. Army Corps of Engineers. These maps generally are available throughout the country and will reveal a particular parcel's susceptibility to flooding.

Find out how stormwater runoff will be handled. Your engineering firm should be consulted to determine any potential drainage problems. The impervious surfaces created by streets, drives, and roofs on a steeply sloped site may cause flooding problems downstream. In such cases, extensive collection and detention systems may be needed. Stormwater runoff can be especially expensive to handle if there is no discharge point close to your site.

Soils

If soils reports have been prepared on the site you are considering, you need to get copies. Expansive clays and silt can be extremely troublesome. Are there any fault

Figure 3.2 Inefficient lot yield

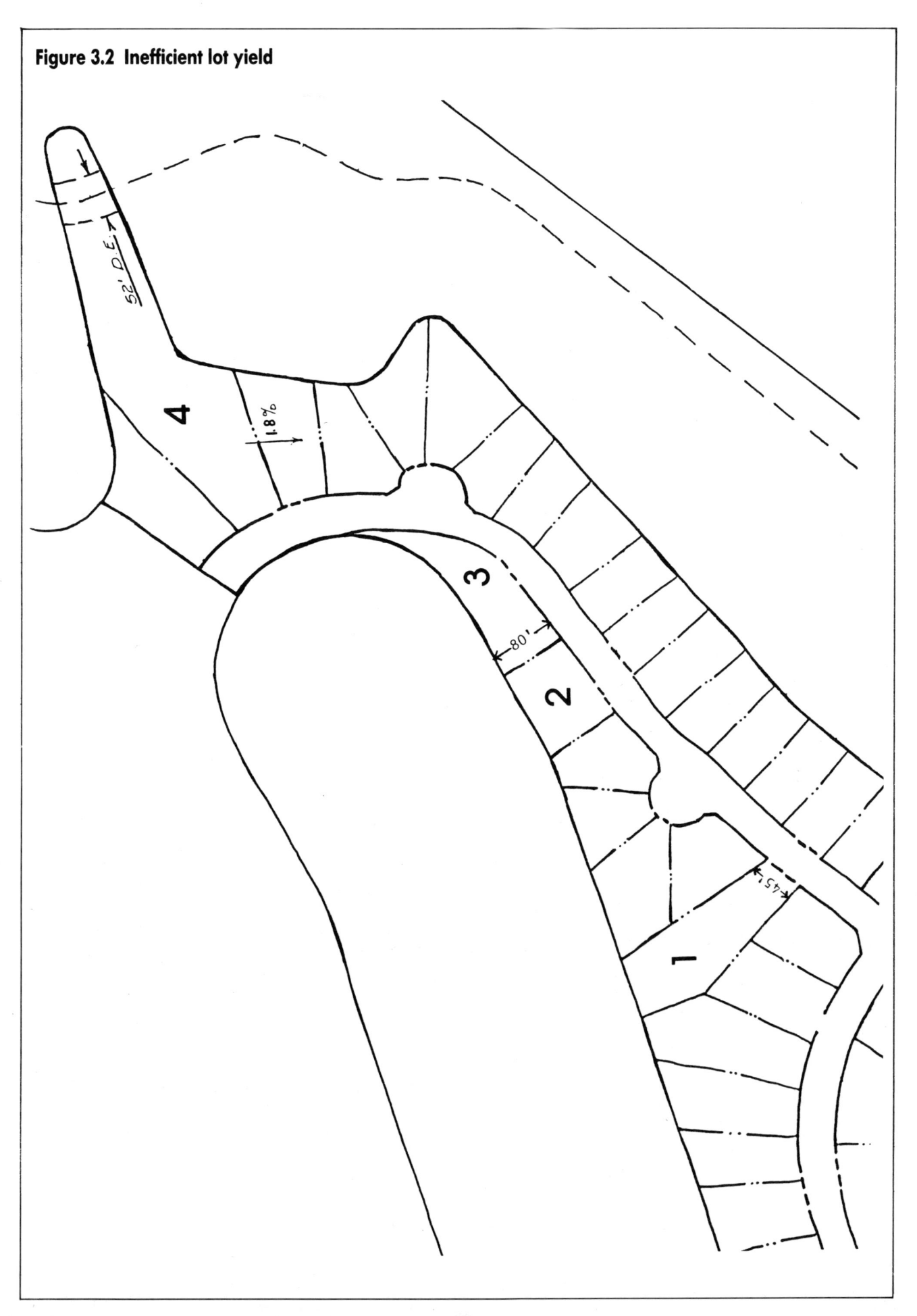

Figure 3.2 Inefficient lot yield

43

lines in the parcel that would make it unsuitable for building? In addition to the standard core drilling tests that have been used for many years, some developers are now using seismic tests to determine the composition of the substrata on a parcel of land.

Given the potential liability exposure of builders/developers for structural failures due to unstable soils, it is extremely important to obtain soils tests. If the site has substantial amounts of unstable soils, it is probably a good idea to reject it. Your potential liability could exceed any potential profits.

Is the site full of rocks? If it is, chances are the rocks continue below the surface. Extensive blasting operations would then be required for construction of the onsite road and utility improvements, and for construction of the residences as well.

Another example of a soil type that presents extreme problems is lava flow covered by a few inches of topsoil. Such a site is literally useless for development because of the enormous cost of hauling and compacting fill dirt to create a buildable site. Other examples of unbuildable sites would be where the water table is exceptionally high, or where a bog underlayment is present.

Vegetation

What costs will be incurred in clearing the land? Is the site heavily forested, or is it grassland? If the site is forested, clearing costs must be included in your development cost estimates. The cost of clearing trees is partially offset by the aesthetic value of large specimen trees that can be isolated and left for the enjoyment of future residents.

Easements and Encroachments

You need a survey of the site that shows any and all easements and encroachments both recorded and unrecorded, both on the surface and below the surface of the parcel. You may also want to have the corners of the parcel staked so you can tell exactly where the boundaries of the property run, and the relationship of those boundaries to the topography and any natural barriers.

Easements will often directly affect your ability to maximize the yield from the parcel. For example, suppose a powerline ran through the middle of a parcel. In order to make the site suitable for development, you might have to pay to have the line moved, create a new easement, and have the utility company vacate the old easement. If the line could not be moved, the yield of the lots might fall because in effect you would be dealing with two sites instead of one. As you physically inspect parcels, you will probably see any overhead powerlines and should assume that easements (recorded or unrecorded) exist below those powerlines. Subsurface easements can be uncovered only by examining the plat and any subsequent recorded easements, or by obtaining a survey that reflects those recorded easements. Typical subsurface easements include those for gas pipelines and sewer lines.

Unrecorded, or prescriptive, easements are created by continuous use of the parcel by another party—a use that may be adverse to your possession. Such a situation arises when an owner of a landlocked piece of ground has been driving across someone else's land to get to his land. In this example, a rutted road leading to the landlocked parcel would be evidence of a prescriptive easement. Even if there is no roadway leading to a landlocked piece abutting your parcel, an easement by necessity may have been created, whereby the owners of the landlocked piece can use your parcel to access theirs. There are also many cases where "squatters" build houses on land owned by others. Squatters do have rights and may be difficult or impossible to evict. Make sure your survey reveals all existing structures and roadways.

Encroachments occur where structures overlap property boundary lines. If there are encroachments, you will have to negotiate with the encroaching party to determine if they will tear the structure down, or if they would be willing to purchase the land underneath it. Encroachments are clouds on the title and must be removed before you can close on the acquisition and development loan.

Deed Restrictions

Obtain a copy of the Schedule B included in the most recent owner's title policy for review. If you do enter into a purchase agreement you will want to have a title commitment issued to you immediately upon execution of the purchase agreement. The Schedule B given to the current owner when he/she bought the property will give you a head start in identifying any title problems. Schedule B (Figure 3.3) lists all the exceptions to the title of the parcel. Often it will refer to a book and page number in the county records. Make sure you review any documents referenced in Schedule B. The easement referenced in Section 11(b) of the Schedule B shown in Figure 3.3, for example, covers the entire parcel!

At the same time, obtain a copy of the current deed for review. Restrictions can appear either in the form of recorded restrictive covenants, or on the face of the deed itself. You must make sure that there is nothing in any of these restrictions that will prevent you from building the type of project you are considering. This is particularly important when you are dealing with multifamily projects, or with housing exceeding normal single-family densities.

Restrictions can take many forms, including restrictions on the permitted uses of a parcel, as well as restrictions on the type of building that can be constructed on the parcel. Height, setback, and architectural restrictions are common.

Restrictive covenants can be broken through court action. If it would be necessary to break covenants to proceed with your project, consult an attorney for an estimate of the time and expense involved in an attempt to break the covenants. There is no guarantee that the court would grant your request. As a general rule, avoid the time and trouble of attempting to break restrictive covenants. Other sites are usually available that are not hampered by such problems. Don't think that because the zoning is correct for what you want to build on the site, the covenants do not count. Zoning and covenants are two separate issues and both must be addressed.

Liens

A lien is an encumbrance or claim that another party has against the parcel. Ask the seller for all liens that exist against the parcel in question. Ask the seller which liens he/she will pay off and which will transfer with the land.

Special assessment district liens reflect the cost of offsite improvements, and are created by the county or city. They cover a specific geographic area that will "benefit" from the installation of roadways, storm sewer, water, and sanitary sewer. Creation of the district allows the city or county to file liens against adjacent parcels of ground. In turn, these liens collateralize bonds that are issued by the city or county and sold to investors. Proceeds from the sale of the bonds pay for the improvements, and—because the issuer is a local government—the interest is tax-exempt. Many developers find it advantageous to request the creation of a special assessment district because the offsite improvement costs are funded initially by someone else, and because the interest cost to the developer is generally lower than other available interest rates. The question you must ask the seller is whether the special assessment district lien is included in the price, or would be assumed by you.

The effect of assuming a special assessment district lien is to increase the total cost of the parcel. For example, if the road is already in, you probably did not provide for the cost of its installation in your initial review of development costs. By assuming the lien, however, you take on the obligation to pay for the offsite development cost plus the land price. Usually you should avoid paying off special assessment district liens if possible. Either assume the lien or have the seller pay for it. If you need new financing at the time of your closing, the lender will require full payment of the special assessment district lien to provide the lender with a first lien position.

Other liens, such as mechanic's liens and judgment liens, must be paid in full before closing on the parcel. The title company will search the title for recorded liens. If there are recorded liens other than those you have agreed to assume, funds will be taken from the seller at closing to pay off those liens. However, the title company will assure you only that the recorded liens have been satisfied. Any unrecorded liens or claims of same will not be known to the title company, and therefore you are not insured against them. If work has been performed recently on the site, you must assure yourself that whoever performed the work has been paid in full, so that you know no mechanic's liens can be filed.

The peculiarity with mechanic's liens is that they can be filed within a given time period after work has been performed. This time period varies from one location to

Figure 3.3 Sample Schedule B

Lawyers Title Insurance Corporation
NATIONAL HEADQUARTERS
RICHMOND, VIRGINIA

SCHEDULE __B__ cont'd.

This policy does not insure against loss or damage by reason of the following:

GENERAL EXCEPTIONS:

1. Rights or claims of parties in possession not shown by the public records.
2. Easements, or claims of easements, not shown by the public records.
3. Encroachments, overlaps, conflicts in boundary lines, shortages in area, or other matters which would be disclosed by an accurate survey and inspection of the premises.
4. Any lien, claim or right to a lien, for services, labor or material heretofore or hereafter furnished, imposed by law and not shown by the public records.
5. Community prperty, downer, curtesy, survivership, or homestead rights, if any, of any spouse of the insured.
6. Any titles or rights asserted by anyone including, but not limited to persons, corporations, governments, or other entities, to lands comprising the shores or bottoms of navigable streams, lakes, or land beyond the line of the harbor or bulkhead lines established or change by the United States Government.
7. Unpatented mining claims; reservations or exceptions in patents or in acts authorizing the issuance thereof; water rights, claims or title to water.
8. Taxes or assessments which are not shown as existing liens by the public record.

SPECIAL EXCEPTIONS

9. Taxes for the year 19 82 , and thereafter.

Case Number   IA 24,309tc   Policy Date   March 23, 1982

Policy Number   85 81 098634   Special Exceptions 82

10. Reservations in Patent from the United States of America, recorded in Book 60, page 30 and Book 77, page 152, records Bernalillo County, New Mexico.

11. Existing easements and rights-of-way, including:

    a) Right-of-Way granted to Mountain States Telephone and Telegraph Company, filed June 3, 1931, in Book 117, page 408, records Bernalillo County, New Mexico.

    b) Easement granted to Public Service Company of New Mexico and Mountain States Telephone and Telegraph Company, filed May 7, 1965, in Book D775, page 429, records Bernalillo County, New Mexico.

    c) Twenty-two (22) foot Road Easement as shown in that certain Plat of Ojo Grande Subdivision, filed August 8, 1978, records Bernalillo County, New Mexico.

    d) Road Easement as shown on that certain Survey, by Hugg Surveying, dated May 28, 1980, records Bernalillo County, New Mexico.

(Continued)

12. Any possible assessments for paving, water or sewer assessments which are or might be a lien by law, but which have not yet been filed for record in the office of the County Clerk of Bernalillo County, New Mexico.

13. AGREEMENT DESIGNATING PROPERTY AS SEPARATE PROPERTY dated June 20, 1980, filed March 23, 1982, at 10:46 a.m., as Document No. 82-15143, records Bernalillo County, New Mexico.

14. DEED OF TRUST from William Gross and Sharon Gross, husband and wife, as to an undivided 1/2 interest; and Owen Garretson, a married man, as to an undivided 1/2 interest, to LAWYERS TITLE INSURANCE CORPORATION, dated June 20, 1980, field March 23, 1982, at 10:46 a.m., as Document No. 82-15145, records Bernalillo County, New Mexico.

15. Title to all mineral rights within and underlying the premises, together with all mineral rights and other rights, privileges and immunities relating thereto.

Policy 85 N M (Rev. 2-79) Litho in U.S.A.
Form No. 035-0-085-3002/2

ALTA Owner's Policy-Form B 1970 (Rev. 10-17-70) Copyright 1969

ISSUING OFFICE COPY

---

another, but generally ranges from 90 to 180 days. Thus, you could buy a piece of land, think you have clear title to it, and find that a lien had been filed against the parcel after closing. Clearing that lien from the property would become your responsibility. Although you might have recourse against the seller, you would be involved in a time-consuming and costly procedure.

Mortgages represent the most common form of lien against property. You will want to discuss with the seller whether any existing mortgage liens already in place can be assumed, or if the seller will take back a note and mortgage (purchase money mortgage) for the purchase of the property. These types of liens will be discussed in more detail in Chapters Six and Seven on financing the land purchase.

Mineral Rights

Mineral rights, where there are any, generally run with the land and are rarely split off and sold to a third party. If, however, a third party owns the mineral rights to a site, he/she can exercise those rights at any time and mine the subject site. Obviously this would be devastating to a development program. Make sure you read the U.S. Patent on the particular parcel and examine the documents called out on Schedule B of your title commitment to make sure the mineral rights have not been sold to a third party by way of a recorded instrument.

Government Plans and Regulations

Government plans and regulations have a far greater impact on the development of a parcel and the related costs of development than any other factor. We have already discussed government involvement in providing offsite improvements such as roads, sanitary sewer, water, and storm drainage. Governments are empowered through their charters to protect public health, welfare, safety, and morals. These objectives are achieved partially through regulating land use, which has resulted in comprehensive plans, zoning ordinances, subdivision regulations, and building codes. The difficulty of maneuvering through the maze of local government regulations and associated approvals varies tremendously from one locale to another. At one extreme are cities such as Houston where there are no zoning ordinances and approvals can be obtained quickly; at the other extreme are certain counties in Maryland and California, where approval processes can take many months. It is not uncommon for the subdivision approval process to take two years or longer in states where growth control policies are emphasized. The developer must have sufficient funds for land carrying costs during the approval period, or run the risk of going out of business.

While it is the rare seller who would allow the buyer enough time to obtain all government approvals before closing on a purchase, it is not unreasonable to ask the seller to provide you with a contingency period during which you can obtain preliminary governmental approvals for your proposed project. Again, each locale will have different time requirements. Consult with your engineering firm to determine what approvals will be required, and approximately how long it will take to get those approvals. The approval process can be quite lengthy if the local government needs to publish a notice of public hearing. When a decision is made following a public hearing, wait until the public appeal period has expired before closing. Generally it is advisable to include a contingency period of six months in your purchase agreement.

Oddly enough, lengthy and stringent government regulations can help the building market. A lengthy approval process reduces the supply of housing products on the market. Thus, the chances of rampant overbuilding are diminished. On the other hand, a restricted supply creates higher prices for the consumer. These higher prices reflect the greater carrying costs and development costs associated with this type of government policy, as well as the simple supply/demand relationship where a product in short supply will generally obtain a higher price than one in abundant supply.

Comprehensive Plans

As the name implies, this is a plan the local government adopts regarding the comprehensive use of all land within its jurisdiction. In larger municipalities, this type of plan may apply to sectors within the community. Development of a comprehensive plan can take months, if not years. The plan provides an overall view of large regions or sectors of the community and how the uses of land within those sectors would interrelate. In this manner, the municipality can direct its attention to assuring appropriate mixes of residential, retail, and office facilities; to providing appropriate school facilities; properly sized water, sanitary sewer, and storm drainage facilities; and adequately sized roadways based on the overall usage and densities indicated by the plan.

This overall approach to planning provides advantages to the developer as well as the municipality. Assuming your usage is allowable under such a comprehensive plan, the city-provided infrastructure should be adequate to serve your needs. If an area that you are interested in developing is governed by a comprehensive plan, be sure to pick up a copy of that plan and study it. It will show you where your potential competition will be located.

Two caveats do exist with respect to a comprehensive plan. First, if the parcel you are looking at is currently the subject of—or is part of—a comprehensive plan study, you will probably find that you can do nothing with the site until that study is completed. Thus, you should ask city planning officials whether they are currently undertaking a study on an area that includes your site, or are anticipating launching such a study in the near future. Because of the popularity of comprehensive plans, this is a very real concern. As we have already discussed, unforeseen time delays can be disastrous to the developer. City administrators will have little empathy if you purchase a piece of ground and subsequently discover that you cannot proceed until a comprehensive plan is completed.

Secondly, make sure that you understand the approval process for development plans in areas covered by a comprehensive plan. Some cities are requiring submission of complete development plans for new projects. Often these development plans must be reviewed at a public hearing before the developer is allowed to proceed. This public review occurs even if the development plan is clearly within the allowable densities stated in a previously-approved comprehensive plan. The public review process is particularly likely to occur where densities are greater than four dwelling units per acre.

The very nature of a public hearing is fraught with potential problems and delays. Cities all across the country are fostering neighborhood groups that—from a developer's point of view—seem determined to prohibit all developments with proposed densities that exceed the densities in the group members' neighborhoods. Even if city administrators state that they will support your development plan, be cautious. Strong neighborhood groups frequently appeal decisions that are favorable to developers of proposed projects and, in many instances, have filed lawsuits in an attempt to block development. As we stated earlier in this chapter, make sure that your purchase agreement is contingent on getting past the appeal period for city approval of your development plan.

Because comprehensive plans are established to provide an orderly framework for future growth, and because city planning administrators believe that a balance among residential, commercial, and office developments is necessary, you may find it extremely difficult to get the city or local planning department to alter or amend their comprehensive plan. This can be the case even where you are downgrading the use (for example, where you may wish to use a parcel for residential development, although the comprehensive plan indicates that site is to be used for office facilities). Make sure you have the planning department's support for your proposed use.

Zoning Ordinances

Zoning ordinances are laws approved by the local government that regulate the uses of land within the community. Zoning is administered by the local government zoning department, and falls into four broad categories: residential, commercial, industrial, and office. Within these four categories, there are many subheadings that allow for different intensities of use. For example, residential is broken down into several subcategories such as single-family, fourplexes, high-rise apartments, townhouses, and so on. If the site you are considering has existing zoning, and is not subject to any comprehensive plan, you should examine the city zoning ordinances, which are usually published for sale. Also purchase a zoning map to check the exact zoning for the parcel you are considering. Then read the zoning ordinance to determine if the proposed project complies with the existing zoning. Whether or not it complies, it is always a good idea to talk with the city zoning officials regarding your proposed development and determine whether they foresee any potential conflicts.

At times city administrators may wish to change the existing zoning of a site. If they are opposed to your proposed use, even though you are in compliance with the zoning, they can create many obstacles in the development process. On the other hand, they may encourage you to ask for a change of zoning if you need one. This will require a public hearing.

If your proposed development is within the allowed provisions of the zoning ordinance, usually you can proceed with getting plans drawn and obtaining a building permit. The building permit procedure generally requires approval by the zoning department, but no public hearing.

An exception to this rule occurs where there is special use zoning or zoning that requires a public hearing and a development plan (such as a PUD). Special use zones were created to enable the planning department to review all development plans and to allow the public to know what those plans are in advance of city approval. The special use designation also allows the developer to avoid compliance with other zoning ordinances, such as those relating to setback and height requirements. Special use designation requires approval of the entire development plan, including all items that would, under standard zoning ordinances, require a special exception. The problems with special use zoning are similar to the problems encountered under a comprehensive plan: there will be delays involved with setting public hearing dates and getting on agendas.

The discussion with zoning or planning officers regarding your proposed development cannot be neglected. Under most zoning ordinances, uses that are less intense than those allowed under the existing zoning can be approved as a conditional use. In the case cited above regarding a residential use on an office-zoned parcel, you might have considerable difficulty obtaining approval under a comprehensive plan. If the site is not included in a comprehensive plan, however, you usually can apply for a conditional use and obtain an approval more easily. The conditional use process normally requires a published hearing, open to the public. Therefore, a conditional use has all the risks associated with a public hearing.

Obtaining variances from zoning ordinance requirements regarding setbacks, height restrictions, and the like can be difficult. If the variance has to be approved by the city zoning officer, you may find the officer is reluctant to approve some variances without reviewing an overall development plan. This review would typically take place at a public hearing. In that event you may be better off to apply for a special use zone and go through a review process similar to that required under a comprehensive plan, rather than experience the delay of waiting for a denial from a zoning officer first, and then appealing that denial. At times, straightforward zoning can be advantageous compared to a comprehensive plan or special use zone.

At other times the comprehensive plan or special use zone has advantages over straight zoning. The discussions with the city zoning and planning department should allow you to proceed with some feeling of confidence regarding the city's position on your proposed development. Again, public hearings are the biggest risk factors, particularly in already well developed areas.

Subdivision Regulations

After municipal planning and/or zoning departments have approved your project, the next hurdles are the locality's subdivision regulations. Many communities have subdivision or development procedural manuals available for purchase. You may wish to obtain these manuals; however, they are highly technical and your civil engineering firm should already own them.

Subdivision regulations set standards for the construction of all onsite improvements, including streets, curbs and gutters, walkways, drainage facilities, sanitary sewer, water, and required easements. Your civil engineering consultant will prepare the layout of your subdivision or apartment project by using a plat map. The plat map will show the locations of all lots, the numbers of the lots and blocks, all streets, and the names of the streets. A plat map may be required before approval is granted by the planning or zoning department.

In addition, the civil engineering firm will prepare working drawings that include required easements from the various utility companies, construction detailing and placement of curbs and gutters, roadways, sidewalks, drainage facilities, and sanitary sewer and water. An important part of the drainage plan will be a grading plan for the site.

The design of these onsite improvements will have an impact on their costs. Requirements for streets, curbs, gutters, walkways, and drainage may vary greatly from one community to another; development costs may vary correspondingly. If you are working in a new community, do not attempt to use cost figures from the community in which you are currently working.

Make sure that lots will be sized to allow sufficient space for the product you intend to build, and to accommodate the required setbacks. Keep in mind that either restrictive covenants or zoning ordinances can create these setback requirements; the more stringent of the two will govern.

The process of subdivision approval involves many city departments as well as public utility companies. Talk to your civil engineering firm about the normal length of time it takes to get these approvals, and make sure that you allow for the costs you will incur carrying the land. The period subsequent to receiving preliminary city approvals will probably be your responsibility to carry—not the seller's.

A number of other signatures may be required on the plat before it is approved and recorded. Among them may be the following city or county departments: traffic, water, sewerage, fire, planning, zoning, environmental, parks and recreation, police, refuse removal, transit, and flood control departments; school districts; and the councils of governments.

Building Codes

Subdivision regulations affect land development, while building codes govern the construction of structures. Building codes affect the total cost of the finished product, and vary considerably from community to community, especially in relation to depth of frostlines and earthquake zones. Be sure to take this into account in cost estimates.

Value Analysis

Because the site factors and government regulations affecting each land parcel are different, the raw land cost of different parcels cannot be compared by relating that cost to a single factor such as the number of dwelling units per acre. From the retail value of the finished lots subtract:

- Cost of onsite and offsite improvements
- Land carrying costs (interest) from purchase to completion of development
- Profit and overhead

The amount that is left is the "residual value" of the raw land. Paying more for the raw land than its residual value will force you to either cut your profit margin or ask a higher-than-market price for the finished product. (This procedure also can be used as a negotiating tool to show the seller what his/her land is worth.)

There will be times when the relationships between raw land cost, profit margin, and value of the finished lots will fluctuate during negotiations. These fluctuations may reflect non-economic factors. Although you should heed the sage's advice to avoid falling in love with the land, you may need the land for other reasons—for example, to gain a foothold in a particular market. It is difficult to assign a dollar value to such a reason when evaluating a parcel.

A footnote on estimating the retail value of the lots and the cost of development: comparisons with similar projects and consultations with appraisers can help verify the estimated retail value of the finished lots and the expected development costs per dwelling unit. Eventually you will need the appraised value of the finished lots for your acquisition-and-development loan approval, so you may as well obtain it at this time.

Land Valuation Example

Assume that each of three land parcels is available for development as a single-family subdivision. The value of a finished lot is $30,000, and there are no locational differences that would justify a premium price on any of the three sites. The asking price for Site A is $25,000/acre; Site B, $25,000/acre; and Site C, $15,000/acre. Figure 3.4 shows a comparative value analysis of the three sites.

Dwelling units/acre Site C is clearly the least expensive, but will yield only two and one-half sites per acre, while each of the other sites will yield three. Site C still has the lowest cost per dwelling unit at $6,000.

Offsite costs Offsite costs also vary. Site A has a contiguous road system and existing sewer and water systems that could handle the demand of the proposed subdivision. Site B would require paving of an existing dirt road at a cost of $20,000. Existing sewer and water lines are not adequately sized for anticipated demand, so there would be an additional $140,000 expense for utility extensions. Site C is bounded by a major unimproved arterial. To obtain development permits, the municipality requires developers to pay for improving a portion of the arterial, and to pay and install sewer and water lines in the arterial that would serve the subject site. Road costs are estimated at $160,000, and sewer and water at $120,000.

Onsite costs Onsite costs of Sites A and B would be $7,000 per lot, but increased grading costs for Site C caused by its irregular terrain push its onsite development cost to $9,000 per lot.

Figure 3.4 Comparative Land Value Analysis

	Parcel A	Parcel B	Parcel C
Total acreage	12	16	20
Dwelling units possible per acre	3	3	2.5
Total dwelling units (lots) in parcel	36	48	50
Total value of finished lots at $30,000 each	$1,080,000	$1,440,000	$1,500,000
Less development costs and profit			
Offsites			
road	-0-	20,000	160,000
sewer and water	-0-	140,000	120,000
Onsites (hard and soft costs) at $7,000 per lot	252,000	336,000	350,000
Extraordinary onsite hard cost	-0-	-0-	100,000
Interest during development period	110,000	143,000	160,000
Profit and overhead (33% of value of finished lots)	360,000	480,000	500,000
Total	772,000	1,119,000	1,390,000
Amount available to purchase land	$ 358,000	$ 321,000	$ 110,000
Asking price of parcel	$ 300,000	$ 400,000	$ 300,000

Carrying costs Interest expense during the development period is calculated at 20 percent of the total cost of land and improvements. This rate is not intended to be a rule-of-thumb, but is merely a quick way of including an interest factor in the calculation of total comparative costs. In reality, interest charges are very changeable and the timing of cash outflows in relation to interest rate changes has a major impact on the total interest bill.

Profit and overhead Profit and overhead are calculated at 33 percent of the proposed sales price.

In this comparison, Site A is clearly the one to select. In fact, the residual value of the land, estimated at $358,000, actually exceeds its cost (asking price of $300,000). A situation where the land's estimated value exceeds its asking price raises a red flag. You may wish to investigate further to make certain you have not overlooked anything. If the initial estimates appear valid, however, Site A represents quite a find—one you are likely to find only as an example in a book.

Site C ostensibly had the least expensive land, but the offsite costs on this particular parcel almost doubled its effective price. Coupled with higher onsite expenses and lower densities (both caused by topography), the estimated residual land value was $110,000. Since this was well below the asking price of $300,000, you would not pursue this parcel.

The lack of readily available road, sewer and water services pushed up the development costs of Site B. The estimated residual land value of $321,000 is $79,000 below the asking price; the sellers might consider an offer at $321,000 if the first choice, Site A, cannot be obtained.

Chapter Four

Organization for Acquisition and Sale

An individual contemplating the acquisition and development of land may decide to operate as a sole proprietor, in a limited or general partnership, or as a corporation.

There are no simple rules regarding which form of business organization is best. Each transaction involves unique legal liabilities and risks, and tax liabilities and benefits. The advice of your attorney and your accountant will be needed to make final decisions. This chapter will outline and define the basic legal business organization structures available to a developer, and broadly indicate their ramifications on land acquisition and development activities.

Sole Proprietorship

Most businesspeople know that one may choose to proceed as an individual sole proprietor, taking personal possession of land titles, acquiring financing, contracting for development, and eventually selling the property in your personal name. Particularly for small-scale projects, this is a good solid method for land acquisition and development activities.

However, the potential impact on your personal financial status must be carefully analyzed. Key questions are whether it would limit your ability to meet family needs or emergencies, whether profits would be diluted by high personal tax rates, and whether the risks inherent in the project justify complete personal financial exposure.

General Partnership

Partnership arrangements are a common form of business organization for land acquisition and development, particularly for larger projects where broader-based ownership structures are needed. Your state's Uniform Partnership Act defines partnership as "the association of two or more persons engaged in business together for profit." Partnerships offer shared risk and shared reward.

The *general partnership* offers relative informality and flexibility, with the opportunity for both (or all) partners to participate in management decisions. In most states partnerships can conduct business in the name of the partnership without permission of the state, can hold title to real property, and constitute separate legal entities with the capacity to sue and be sued.

The general partnership has the advantages of informality and flexibility. Organization and liquidation are relatively simple procedures, and arrangements for capitalization, profit and loss allocation, voting rights, and other issues are straightforward as long as they are covered in the partnership agreement. Tax benefits flow through to the individual partners, and the partnership itself is not taxed.

The major disadvantage of a general partnership is the unlimited liability of the partners. The general partnership is a mutual agency relationship whereby each partner is an agent and a principal. This renders each partner liable for the acts of all other partners in relation to the partnership business.

Another disadvantage is that the law generally requires legal dissolution of general partnerships upon the death or withdrawal of a partner, unless prior agreements preventing this dissolution have been made. Where no prior agreements exist, death or withdrawal can lead to management problems and stalemates among the remaining partners.

Each partner has the power to bind the partnership, and this power alone can present difficulties when there is dissension among the partners. In general partnerships, each partner's interest is nontransferrable.

The basis of a partnership in land acquisition and development should be mutuality of purpose and capability, or complementary abilities and capabilities. The partnership shares or spreads personal risk, but does not eliminate it. Experienced legal as well as financial counsel is absolutely recommended before entering a partnership.

A *joint venture* is a partnership created for one project only, but covers acquisition as well as financing. Joint ventures are discussed in detail in Chapter Six.

A *limited partnership*, when properly structured, affords partners the tax advantages of a partnership or proprietorship, with the personal liability limitation offered by incorporation. The more complex structure creates two partnership classes—the general (managing) partner or partners, and the limited (investing) partner or partners. This structure requires state approval for formation.

The legal liability of a limited partner is limited to his/her actual or committed financial contribution to the partnership. Like general partnerships, limited partnerships can hold title to real estate, constitute separate legal entities, and permit tax deductions to flow through to the individual partners.

Limited partnerships permit centralized management by the general partner(s), which affords the opportunity for more management continuity than with the general partnership. The death, bankruptcy, or withdrawal of a limited partner would not trigger dissolution of the partnership. Unless continuation provisions are included in the limited partnership agreement, however, similar circumstances involving a general partner would dissolve the partnership.

Transfer of financial interest in a limited partnership is relatively easy, but must be carefully structured to avoid tax problems. Since transferability is a characteristic of corporations, partnerships organized to closely resemble a corporate form are sometimes taxed as corporations (see **Avoiding Tax Problems** below).

Tax benefits are among the most well known benefits of limited partnerships. The tax benefits pass through to all the partners, including the limited partners, and the partnership itself is not taxed.

Public disclosure requirements are a disadvantage of the limited partnership form, particularly where investors want to protect their financial privacy. Upon formation or transfer of a partnership interest, certificates must be filed in public offices. Securities regulations may also require the general partner to produce and distribute lengthy and detailed disclosure statements upon the marketing and sale of limited partnership interests.

Avoiding Tax Problems

As noted above, partnerships that are structured to closely resemble corporations may be subject to corporation taxes.

Current IRS requirements state that if a partnership has *no more than two* of the following characteristics, it will not be taxed as a corporation:

- Continuity of life
- Centralization of management
- Limitation of liability
- Free transferability of interest

Corporation

The corporation is probably the most widely used business structure for the acquisition and development of large land parcels.

The clearest advantages of the corporation form are that it insulates the participants from personal liability and permits free transferability of stock interest. The corporation allows an individual or a group to conduct business without personal participation in the risk, but full participation in the rewards.

Corporations are separate legal entities capable of holding title to real estate, but are also subject to taxation. Their major disadvantage is that distribution of profit may be characterized by the IRS as dividends and, as such, taxed twice. The corporation pays corporate tax on its income, and the recipient of corporate dividends also pays taxes on dividends received. Unlike salaries, dividends are not deductible to the corporation.

Forming corporations is expensive, and corporations are subject to more state and local regulatory control than other business entities. The incorporator(s) are required to register with the state. Articles of incorporation and annual reports must be filed by a registered agent of the corporation. Initial and annual incorporation fees and franchise taxes are levied by the state of incorporation and any other states in which the corporation does business.

There is no need to advise you to seek legal counsel, because in most states you will need a lawyer to set up your corporation and assist in its maintenance. An accountant will also be needed to set up independent books for the corporation. In some circumstances it is possible to have your corporation taxed as a partnership if you find this desirable. (Your lawyer can give you information on this arrangement, called the "Subchapter S" corporation.)

The corporate structure allows very clear definitions of ownership and responsibility. Management is centralized, and the shareholders, if any, have practically no direct control over the affairs of the corporation. Like partnerships, corporate structures have the benefit of bringing together complementary abilities and capabilities. Developers have been known to start a separate corporation for each new land development project.

Summary

Whether you structure your project as a sole proprietorship, a limited or general partnership, or a corporation, your choice should be made after careful consideration of your specific needs, and with the best available legal and financial advice. The decision will be dependent on many factors, including the method of purchase and the form of financing. Formation of partnerships and corporations is itself a method of financing, or at least of acquiring working capital for a project.

Chapter Five
Methods for Acquisition

So far in this book we have covered market research, community and neighborhood analysis, and evaluation of potential development sites. We have discussed business organization for acquisition and development of real estate. Now we are ready to discuss actual land acquisition.

The seller's needs and desires in most cases determine the method you, as the purchaser, will use in your acquisition, unless you intend to pay cash. At one extreme are the sellers who will take only cash; at the other are those who will defer payments until you develop the land, build a product, and sell it. But the most common selling arrangements involve a 20-25 percent downpayment, with the balance financed through a land loan.

Standard Land Purchase Contract

Appendix 5-A shows an example of a standard land purchase contract. Note that the provisions and riders to the contract not only define the agreement for the transfer of the property title, but effectively describe how the acquisition is financed. Chapters Six and Seven cover land financing in more detail.

Not all buyers have cash available, or want to spend available cash for a downpayment. It is often possible to combine a deferral of part of the payment to the seller (all or part of the downpayment) with other financing to make an acquisition work for both the buyer and seller. If you can agree on most of the terms of your contractual agreement but find a few issues that cannot be resolved without an investment of time and money, or that rest on municipal decisions (as discussed in Chapter Three), a *contingency contract* may serve your needs.

Contingency Contract

A contract that contains contingency clauses establishes all the terms of the purchase, but does not bind the parties until the specified contingencies are met. A contingency is a condition that must be met before the buyer is obligated to proceed. A contingency clause might read as follows:

- *The buyer's obligations under this Agreement are contingent upon seller's provision of percolation test results and soil bore results satisfactory to buyer and buyer's engineer, on or before May 15, 19XX.*

Or,

- *The buyer shall present an application for zoning Property in accordance with the attached Land Plan to the City Council of Yourtown, Ohio on or before January 15, 19XX. In the event buyer has not obtained final approval for such zoning or for other zoning, acceptable to buyer in buyer's sole discretion on or before October 15, 19XX, then, upon written notice to seller, this contract shall become null and void and all earnest monies, together with interest accrued thereon, shall be returned to buyer and buyer shall have no further obligation hereunder.*

Issuance of building permits or securing financing are other common examples of contingencies. (See also Appendix 5-D, paragraphs 11-12.)

Option or Option Contract

The goal of remaining unbound until all contingencies have been met can also be served with an *option*, or *option contract*. An option is a commitment from the seller that you, the buyer, may purchase the property *if you want to*, on certain conditions, and generally for a specific price and on or before a specific date. For the option to be of value to you and the seller, the conditions of sale must be very clearly stated. Appendix 5-B shows an example of an option contract.

The option contract is very similar to a contingency contract; in some cases they are identical. In some cases, a contingency contract may be more palatable to a seller than an option. In others, an option contract can be a very effective method of meeting both buyers' and sellers' needs during negotiations. As a buyer, an option contract gives you a secure agreement, subject only to events or timing that neither seller or buyer can control or predict.

Option contracts are widely used as financing tools (see Chapter Six).

Land Installment Contract

Appendix 5-C shows an example of a *Land Installment Contract*. Under this type of an agreement, the owner retains title (and possibly possession and use) of the land until the purchase price is fully paid. This type of an agreement often permits phased release of portions of the land, with perhaps 20 percent of the land held by the seller until full payment of a three- to four-year contract. If the seller is retaining possession, farming and other present uses may continue. The arrangement provides the seller with security and enables the buyer to obtain release of at least a majority of the land that is paid for.

In an installment sale, the purchaser contracts to make periodic payments to the seller with interest on the unpaid portion of the purchase price, until the purchase price is entirely paid and the deed delivered to the buyer. These arrangements usually provide the seller with the right to terminate the agreement if the buyer defaults on payments. In a default, the seller normally cannot force the buyer to buy the remainder of the land. This is a "nonrecourse" contract. In some states, however, an installment seller is allowed an "election of remedies." This permits the seller to choose between forfeiting the contract, reacquiring the land without recourse, or forcing the buyer to pay the remainder and complete the purchase contract. In states allowing the seller election of remedies, the buyer should negotiate for a nonrecourse contract.

If problems with local utility companies or municipal governments are anticipated, a buyer should negotiate for an abatement of periodic payments on a land contract during the time of a utility or building moratorium beyond the control of the purchaser/developer.

It is also important for a buyer to retain the right to pay off the outstanding balance at any time to facilitate land development plans. An early payoff can cause the seller tax problems, however—depending on how it is reported.

Phased Land Purchase Contract

Appendix 5-D shows a phased land purchase contract, under which the purchaser agrees to buy successive parcels of land from the seller in successive closings over an extended time period. As with the installment contract, the buyer should negotiate for nonrecourse provisions that allow the buyer to terminate at any time by forfeiting the right to acquire more parcels. This type of contract can allow a developer to match land acquisition with the pace of development and sales absorption.

Both the installment land purchase contract and the phased land purchase contract are perceived as more advantageous to the purchaser than to the seller, and thus require hard, detailed negotiations with good, experienced legal advice.

Summary

The method of land acquisition is an integral factor in financing. Your legal and financial advisors should assist in the decisions regarding land acquisition methods by providing careful analysis of the sellers' requirements and your specific needs. A well put-together acquisition contract is a definite asset in securing acquisition financing.

Chapter Six

Private Sector Financing Alternatives

The preceding chapters have examined the critical issues involved in analyzing and acquiring land for residential development. Each presents unique challenges to the developer; but in most cases the biggest challenge a developer faces is the need to convince potential financial backers of the merits of a project.

This chapter will discuss various private sector financing alternatives that are the more traditional sources of funding for residential projects. Chapter Seven covers some of the increasingly popular public sector financing alternatives. Chapter Eight gives guidance on selecting a lender and preparing a loan application.

Financing Phases

Because the financial community is fragmented into different institutions specializing in particular segments of the real estate development market—with each segment characterized by a different level of risk—developers typically finance each phase of residential developments separately. The four phases of financing for a typical residential project are:

- Land acquisition financing
- Land development financing
- Construction financing
- Interim financing

This chapter will discuss each of these financing stages separately because each has unique characteristics and requirements. It should be noted, however, that major lending institutions often finance more than one phase of larger, more complex projects.

One result of the high inflation rates in the early 1980s was the emergence of alternative financing sources. It has now become commonplace for developers to seek an additional infusion of equity capital through the syndication of a portion of the equity in a project. Use of sale/leasebacks as a vehicle for increasing financing leverage has also increased. These two approaches will be discussed later in this chapter.

Financing Land Acquisition

Once a residential builder has conducted the necessary market research to determine that there is sufficient demand to support the proposed development, and has located a suitable land parcel, the next challenge is to obtain the necessary financing to secure the site.

Relatively few major institutional lenders are involved in land acquisition financing. Financial institutions have traditionally hesitated to lend money for raw land development because it is considered very risky. Since the raw land will generate no cash flow, the financial institution must rely on the creditworthiness of the developer for assurance that they will receive payment. Raw land may be difficult to resell should the project fail, which reduces its value as collateral.

The institutions that do finance raw land purchases typically provide no more than a 50 to 60 percent loan-to-value ratio, and the proportion of their real estate loan portfolio that can be used for this purpose is restricted.[1] Major financial institutions would be most likely to become involved in this type of financing if the acquisition funds were included as part of the land development financing.

In the absence of conventional financing, the residential developer is faced with five means of alternative financing[2]:

- Purchase money mortgage
- Purchase option

- Long-term lease plus option
- Joint venture
- Interim land loans

Each of these options is discussed below.

Purchase Money Mortgage

The most common means of financing raw land acquisition is through the use of a purchase money mortgage that is taken back by the seller. The developer typically seeks a loan with no amortization, or with the amortization delayed, and asks the seller to agree to subordinate his first mortgage on the land to a subsequent construction financing lender. Most construction lenders demand first liens.

Under the terms of a purchase money mortgage, the seller of the land accepts, in lieu of cash, the developer's note for the unpaid price of the land secured by a mortgage on the property being sold. This approach creates immediate financing for the developer and creates an investment for the seller secured by his or her own property. In return for this highly advantageous financing opportunity for the buyer, the seller receives a higher return than would be expected from a financial institution.

Purchase money mortgage agreements often require the developer to pay a minimum of 10 percent downpayment. The mortgage term is generally fairly short, although the purchaser often does not want to pay the high monthly costs associated with a shorter term. Balloon payments are often used, where monthly payments are set on a 20- to 30-year schedule, but the loan matures in 10 years with the unpaid balance paid as a lump sum at the end. Prepayment of the purchase money financing is common and is generally favorable to both the buyer and seller as soon as development has progressed to the point that conventional financing is available.

The purchase money mortgage represents a very reasonable approach for financing land acquisition, but requires a land owner who can benefit from the transaction and is willing to take the risks involved.

Purchase Option

Options are among the most widely used techniques for securing control of land parcels for subsequent development. Under an option agreement, the developer purchases the right to control a given parcel while deciding whether to develop the land. The option allows the developer to assemble multiple land parcels for a comparatively small cash outlay, and, in the case of longer-term options, provides a vehicle for speculating on the future value of the land. Should the developer decide not to proceed with the project, it may be possible to resell the option to another developer at a profit.

Several different types of options are often used, including:[3]

Fixed Option This allows the developer to purchase the property for a fixed price during the established option period.

Step-up Option For long-term options where the purchase price of the property increases in stages, often at the time of the option renewal.

Rolling Option This approach is widely used by subdividers as a means of moving in sequence from one track to another as the development progresses. Often the price of the land in later tracts rises as property value increases.

Full Credit Option In this instance, the price of the option is fully credited against the purchase price of the land if the transaction moves forward.

Declining Credit Option As an incentive to shorten the option period, the proportion of the option that can be credited to the purchase price declines over time.

The option process provides the residential developer with a means of controlling the land during the time he/she is seeking financing for the actual property purchase. It is often used as a first step in conjunction with other financing techniques.

Long-Term Lease Plus Option

Under a long-term lease plus option, the developer offers the land owner a lease, with an option to purchase during the lease term. This approach offers the developer two advantages: payments under the lease will be treated as rent, and are therefore deductible; and nonpayment of the rent will not result in an automatic termination of the agreement, since the landowner would have to institute a legal action. Again, the feasibility of the approach depends on the seller's willingness to enter into this type of agreement.

Joint Venture

Joint ventures with landowners, or third parties, are an increasingly popular method of securing control of the land and/or carrying out the development. The partner can be a full participant making equity contributions, and sharing in the proportional losses and gains of the project, or may take a more passive or subordinate role. Joint ventures will be discussed more fully later in this chapter in the section on equity financing.

The principal advantage that joint ventures offer the developer is that payments to the landowner may be delayed until the project begins to generate cash flow. In return for this deferral, the landowner may be able to negotiate a share in the venture larger than that dictated by the value of the land contribution. The proportion of the joint venture controlled by the landowner is often 35 to 55 percent, depending on the degree of risk assumed by each party.

Interim Land Loans

Some private sector loan companies and other lenders specialize in short-term loans on vacant land. These loans are nonamortizing, are at comparatively high interest rates, and are made for 50 percent or less of the appraised value of the land. Since these loans need to be subordinated to secure construction financing, additional collateral is often necessary to secure an interim land loan.

A third party may provide the necessary credit to permit an institutional lender to make a loan to a developer. Under this approach, the primary lender must be satisfied with the credit-worthiness of the second lender.

The secondary lender may support the loan through either an absolute guarantee of repayment, an absolute purchase of the loan from the primary lender, or a take-out commitment to buy the loan for a specified amount at a specific time. The take-out commitment is generally preferred by secondary lenders.

Land Development Financing

Once a developer has acquired the land for a project, the next financing milestone is to obtain financing for land development. Land development financing covers the following activities:

- Site preparation
- Installation of infrastructure (streets, sewers, etc.)
- Engineering and consultants
- Architect fees
- Zoning
- Other soft costs

At this stage the developer is seeking financing to begin to increase the value of the raw land. Lending for land development is considered a high risk venture since the increased value will not occur if the project fails.

Most land development loans represent a first lien on the property, are short-term, and involve interest rates 3 to 4 points above prime. Land development loans are made separately from construction loans when the raw land must be subdivided into smaller lots. They are considered riskier than construction loans because repayment of the development loan is contingent on the sale of building sites. Construction loans are generally backed by a commitment from the builder to assume the loan if the product does not sell.

Lenders making land development loans are primarily concerned with the creditworthiness of the developer and the feasibility and profitability of the project. In making decisions on applications for land development loans, lenders evaluate a variety of factors related to the project, which are discussed further in Chapter 8. Some of the documents commonly required in the application are:[4]

- Current financial statements for the borrower
- Feasibility/market studies
- Appraisal reports
- Physical surveys of the land
- Site plans
- Area demographic studies
- Aerial photographs
- Environmental impact statement
- Estimates of hard and soft development costs

The repayment to the lender is generally accomplished through a "release price" procedure. The release price per lot is calculated based on the proportion of the project's total financing cost represented by the lot, plus 10 to 20 percent. The use of 110 to 120 percent of the proportional share is required by lenders to minimize the risk associated with the development: it allows the lender to recapture the bulk of the loan before project close-out. This procedure allows the developer to receive his/her profit from the sale of the lots at the end of the development period, which provides the lender with further assurance.

The first step in obtaining land development financing involves preparation of a loan offer for submission to the lender's loan committee. This offer typically includes:[5]

- Borrower's name and address
- Amount of the loan
- Term of the loan
- Interest rate on the loan
- Commitment fee charged to make the loan
- Primary purpose of the loan
- Guarantors' names and a short summation of their net worth; a breakdown of their asset holdings; and descriptions of their background and projected annual net income
- Collateral for the loan
- Location of the property to be developed
- Description of the development plan
- Summary of estimated development costs
- Marketing plan
- Projected sales breakdown
- Provisions for release of sold lots
- Other loan conditions
- Recommendation regarding whether the loan should be made

Chapter Eight gives guidance on negotiating with lenders and preparing loan applications.

To minimize the risks involved in larger, more complex projects, lenders often require a phased disbursement approach for financing. The developer builds only immediately marketable products, and changes the product to address the needs of changing markets as the development progresses. This approach limits the lender's liability for a particular project to the phase currently under development. To further assure repayment of land development loans, developers are frequently required to post a performance and payment bond with personal guarantees by the developer as a condition of obtaining financing.[6]

Even with all these performance requirements the lending community considers land development financing risky. Lenders generally also require some connection to the eventual end-financing for the project, so that they are assured of repayment. An eventual take-out commitment, a strong record of sales, and strong developer equity are the key ingredients in a successful application.

Because these loans are perceived as somewhat less risky than straight land acquisition loans, institutional lenders are more willing to lend. Among the institutional lenders, commercial banks and certain savings and loan institutions are most involved in land development financing. The lender's willingness to finance land development is often driven by the desire to be involved in the construction or permanent financing.

Lenders are often willing to lend 70 to 80 percent of the appraised value of the finished lots, as long as that amount does not exceed the costs associated with land acquisition and construction.

Construction Financing

The next step in the residential development process is to secure construction financing. Many institutional lenders are involved in this type of lending. A brief overview is presented below; more detail is provided in Chapter Eight, which covers selection of a lender.

Sources of Construction Financing

The Urban Land Institute recently completed an analysis of 518 construction loans from around the nation made from the second to the fourth quarter of 1984. As Figure 6.1 shows, commercial banks make the majority of construction loans (51.8 percent), and savings and loans make 20.5 percent. A variety of sources account for the remainder of construction loans—life insurance companies, syndicators, mortgage bankers, etc.

Figure 6.1
SOURCES OF CONSTRUCTION FINANCING

Total Loan Amounts
(Millions of Dollars)

	All Loans	Percent Total	New Const.	Percent Total
Total Loans	$6,412	100.0%	$6,184	100.0%
Banks	$3,324	51.8%	$3,243	52.4%
Savings & Loans	1,316	20.5	1,264	20.4
Public Financing*	157	2.5	12	92.1
Life Insurance	586	9.1	579	9.4
Mortgage Bankers	316	4.9	298	4.8
Savings Banks	255	4.0	238	3.8
Credit Companies	139	2.2	129	2.1
Syndications	64	1.0	58	0.9
Internal Funding	49	0.8	46	0.7
REITs	58	0.9	54	0.9
Wall Street Firms	101	1.6	101	1.6
Foreign Lenders	46	0.7	46	0.7

*"Public Financing" refers to any tax-exempt loan or public loan

Source: Urban Land Institute, *Dollars and Percents of Development Financing 2-4 Quarter, 1984*

Characteristics of Construction Financing

The major characteristics of construction financing are:[7]

Short term The term of the loan is usually set to cover the expected period of construction—usually from six months to three years. The lenders in the residential segment of the financial community expect payment in full at the end of the construction period. For commercial projects, construction financing can evolve into permanent financing.

Funds disbursed as construction progresses The funds derived from a construction loan are released as construction progresses, in a predetermined sequence. The developer pays interest on only the funds disbursed, and the lender's risk is reduced since the outstanding loan is matched closely to the value of construction.

Repayment at maturity During the construction period there is no cash flow and no amortization on the loan. Repayment is required at maturity, usually from the proceeds of long-term financing or from sale of the residential units.

High loan-to-value ratio Construction loans generally equal 100 percent of the total construction cost if the developer can provide adequate security or a take-out commitment equal to the construction cost.

Take-out commitment required The construction lender typically requires a first mortgage on the land and construction in place, as well as an assurance of repayment through a take-out commitment for a permanent lender or an equity purchaser.

High interest rates Because of the risk involved and the ongoing administrative burden, construction loans involve relatively high interest rates and substantial loan commitment fees.

Risks of Construction Lending

Construction and land development lending share a unique set of risks associated with the real estate market.

First, loans must be made based on estimates, projections, and judgments rather than facts. Lenders must assess the project's marketability, the accuracy of construction cost estimates, and the developer's competence—and none of these crucial factors is a known entity. In addition, construction projects are subject to many external factors that can dramatically affect their success, including:

- Weather delays
- The unavailability of scheduled land
- Material shortages
- Environmental and other regulatory barriers
- Changes in market demand

Lenders attempt to minimize risk by controlling these factors as much as possible. An understanding of the lender's viewpoint helps developers in negotiations with lenders. More guidance on preparing loan applications is provided in Chapter Eight.

Loan Disbursements

Once the loan agreement is signed, the lender and developer must follow a very strict loan disbursement process. Funds are made available as work progresses. General contractors are frequently required to authorize payouts, but payments are issued directly to subcontractors to assure their receipt of funds. Lenders conduct frequent inspections to make certain that the work is proceeding according to plan and the funds are being disbursed properly.

The Take-out Commitment

Lenders of construction funding for residential properties often require a take-out commitment, which is an agreement by the builder to assume the permanent loan directly if the house is not sold within one year of the commitment date. The loan to the builder would be at the same ratio as the construction loan—usually 80 percent of the sales value of the house—but the rate would be higher and the term shorter than that offered an occupant buyer. The builder still faces the problem of selling the house, but is responsible only for a monthly payment rather than immediate repayment of the full amount of the construction loan; and the construction lender receives full payment. A wide variety of take-out commitments are available to residential developers. The major differences are duration, interest rates, and costs.[8]

Commitment Duration

While typical take-out commitments are a year in duration, the time frame can vary, depending on the characteristics of the project, the market, and the lender's motivation.

Builders need to balance conflicting objectives when negotiating take-out commitments. In inflationary markets, it is advantageous to lock in the interest rates as long as possible. The length of the commitment determines its cost, however, so builders also have a stake in minimizing cost by keeping the loan period short. A rule-of-thumb is to seek a commitment for several months longer than one expects to need it, to provide a cushion in the event of unexpected project delays or other circumstances that would push the project beyond the commitment period—such as buyers that are unable to sell their existing residence. Developers often try to coordinate the start of their commitments with the beginning of actual construction.

Commitment Rate

There are a variety of approaches to setting the interest rate on a take-out commitment. Under a fixed-rate commitment, all loans are at a specified rate. If interest rates are higher than the commitment rate—say 12 percent versus the commitment at 10 percent—the purchasers will use the commitment rate; if they are lower, purchasers will go elsewhere for financing.

It is common practice for forward commitments to fix the rate on the up-side only. For example, the commitment rate might be stated as 12 percent, or the "market rate," whichever is lower at the time of funding. The term "market rate" is often defined using Federal National Mortgage Association (Fannie Mae) or Federal Home Loan Mortgage Corporation (Freddie Mac) rates, or the lending rate of major banks in the area.

A "floating" or "over-the-counter" commitment typically does not specify the interest rate, but states that they will be at the lender's market rate at time of closing, or uses some other index, such as Fannie Mae auction rates. Thus, the floating commitment assures the developer of funds, but does not assure the interest rate. When there is a limited availability of funds, as in the 1974-75 recession, this type of commitment is very valuable.

Commitment Cost

Lenders' charges for commitments are based on their level of risk exposure. Commitments of shorter duration with more flexible rate terms are generally less costly than either lengthy or fixed-rate commitments. At a time of 11 percent interest rates, a commitment for 11 percent financing will be more costly than one at 11.5 or 12 percent. The length of the commitment, which affects the lender's exposure, will also affect cost.

Special Commitment Terms

The commitment will often include special loan terms, such as:[9]
- Establishment of a maximum loan amount
- Maximum lending ratios (i.e., 90 percent on loans up to $100,000; 95 percent on loans up to $125,000, etc.)
- Criteria for qualifying buyers
- Policies regarding investor versus owner/occupant purchasers

- Buy-down policies on the loan
- Pre-sale requirements stipulating that a certain percentage of units must be sold before closing on any loans (this is most common in condominium and PUD projects)

Sources of Commitment Funds

The principal sources of take-out funds are thrift institutions, commercial banks and mortgage bankers. (Chapter Eight gives more information on the differences among lending institutions.)

Interim Financing

Interim financing can be used to provide short-term (usually one to five year) financing to cover the time between construction financing and permanent financing, when construction of the units has been completed but the units have not been sold to owner occupants. The interim financing will pay off the construction loan and finance the carrying cost of the units until their eventual sale, at a lower cost to the developer than if he or she had to pay the full cost of the units.

Interim loans are usually used for newly completed projects. There are several situations where interim financing is used:[10]

During periods of oversupply When a builder cannot sell units because of a temporary over-supply situation, interim financing can enable him/her to carry the costs until the units are absorbed.

Increased demand If rents are escalating rapidly, the developer may want to obtain interim financing until he/she can realize the benefit of the higher rentals.

Leasing dependent on completion Sometimes developers cannot lease completed rental units until the entire project is completed. Interim financing is used to bridge the time gap between construction completion and obtaining permanent financing for the fully leased project.

Mixed-use projects Projects that have many components under development at different times may require interim financing to bridge the time from completion of individual portions of the project until arrangements are made for the permanent financing for the whole project.

Condominium projects Developers of condominium units pay off construction loans from the sale of individual units. If absorption is slow, interim financing can be used until permanent financing is available.

Personal liability If the developer lacks experience in the industry, the lender may want the developer to assume personal liability. Use of interim financing can limit the developer's liability to the period until he/she can obtain nonrecourse financing.

Thus, the use of interim financing gives developers the ability to cope with problems related to the sale of their units that may be out of their control, and to carry the project until permanent financing can be obtained.

Sale and Leaseback Transactions

Due to the complex legal and tax issues involved, it is difficult to present a brief overview of sale/leaseback transactions under the current Internal Revenue Code and case histories. Each transaction must be carefully examined to determine the particular facts and circumstances involved. What follows is a general discussion. Careful legal and accounting analysis is required to assure desired tax treatment.

Advantages

Sale/leaseback transactions can be economically superior to simple mortgage financing for several reasons. The seller/lessee can obtain a tax deduction, in the form of rental payments, equal to 100 percent of the fair market value of the property provided certain requirements of the Internal Revenue Code are met. Also, lenders are generally limited to lending less than 100 percent of the value of property when securing a loan. In a typical sale/leaseback situation, however, the seller/lessee can get 100 percent financing of the project. Because the long-term lease is not booked as indebtedness for most financial accounting purposes, the balance sheet of the seller/lessee retains a better debt-to-equity ratio, which may be important for establishing lines of credit and securing loans for other purposes.

However, it should be noted that a 1976 Financial Accounting Standards Board regulation (Statement of Financial Accounting Standards No. 13) requires a distinction between "capital leases" and "operating leases" for financial accounting purposes. If the lease contains a bargain purchase option and the lease term equals 75 percent or more of the estimated economic life of the leased property, the Financial Accounting Standards Board requires entering the lease as an asset and the rental payments as a liability on the balance sheet.

The biggest single advantage to a seller/lessee has historically been reduced financing cost. This is accomplished by passing depreciation and other tax deductions associated with the property to a party that presumably can make better use of them. However, tax saving opportunities were diminished by the Tax Reform Act of 1986, which reduced depreciation rates and repealed the investment tax credit. Prior to 1986, long-term sale/leaseback financing often reduced the seller/lessee's cost of financing by as much as 600 basis points. (Basis points are one-tenth of one percent of the selling price.)

Disadvantages

There are some disadvantages to the seller/lessee. First, the sale aspect of the transaction can trigger a recapture of depreciation and pre-1986 investment tax credit at the time of the sale. Secondly, there is no prepayment provision or ability to change the implicit interest rate in the lease transaction once the lease term has commenced. The sale/leaseback transaction may restrict expansion where the purchaser/lessor does not wish to cooperate with additional construction plans. Finally, the greatest disadvantage to a seller/lessee is the uncertainty regarding tax treatment that will be discussed below.

If the sale is to a related party, Section 1239(a) of the Internal Revenue Code would require any gain on the sale transaction to be reported as ordinary income, which will be a significant factor through 1987. Generally speaking, sale/leaseback transactions with related parties will not offer the tax benefits that would otherwise be available, although after 1987 when capital gain treatment will be the same as ordinary income, the significance of related party transactions will be decreased.

The Internal Revenue Service (IRS) has taken two approaches in attacking sale/leaseback transactions. First, IRS has maintained in some cases that the transaction constitutes a "like-kind" exchange of properties, and thus is not in fact a sale. Secondly, IRS has maintained that some sale/leaseback transactions constitute a financing device as opposed to true sale and leaseback.

It should be noted that the *Examination Tax Shelters Handbook* for IRS agents indicates that sale and leaseback transactions are to be closely scrutinized for their tax avoidance potential. Agents are advised to request technical advice from the national office when confronted with a sale/leaseback transaction. This facilitates uniform application of the criteria for judging the validity of a sale/leaseback transaction that were established by the U.S. Supreme Court in a 1978 decision. In the case of *United States v. Frank Lyon Co.*,[11] the Supreme Court established a good-faith business purpose test to determine the tax legitimacy of sale/leaseback transactions.

The courts will approach each sale/leaseback transaction on its own particular merits, identify the factors that should be considered in determining the economic substance of the transaction, and then balance the factors. There is no clear guideline as to how these various factors must be weighed, and court decisions are not completely consistent.[12] While sale/leaseback transactions offer the advantages cited above, there is an air of uncertainty since the U.S. Supreme Court decision in the *Lyon* case. For this reason, all sale/leaseback transactions must be measured carefully against the guidelines used by the IRS, and a careful determination should be made regarding the transaction's viability under current law.

Equity Financing

Equity financing can be used for both land acquisition and project construction. However, equity financing often constitutes a larger portion of the total financing package for land acquisition than for construction.

The distinction between debt and equity financing has been blurred in recent years, partially as a result of growing equity participation on the part of investors who were previously involved only in debt lending. These lenders have found that a combination of debt and equity participation is a more attractive investment position in a volatile economy.

The major distinction between the equity and debt positions for any given project is the element of risk. While both positions involve risk, the equity investor assumes the primary risk due to his/her residual interest in the property. All operating costs for the project, and all debts, must be paid before the equity investor realizes any return. In addition, other investors will not suffer any losses until the equity position has been entirely drained.

The most obvious source of equity funding for a project is the developer, but relatively few developers are both capable of and willing to invest substantial amounts of their own funds. Outside sources of capital are usually sought. The primary means of securing equity capital, discussed below, are joint ventures and syndications.

Joint Ventures

A joint venture involves the developer and one or more outside parties who join forces to provide capital and/or expertise for a project. A third party is often involved as a debt partner. The developer provides expertise, and, in some cases, also makes a capital contribution. Pension funds, domestic and foreign investment groups, wealthy individuals, and the service corporations of savings and loan associations often provide capital. Increasingly, savings and loans use internal development subsidiaries to participate in residential joint venture projects. An advantage of a joint venture arrangement with a savings and loan is that it may facilitate negotiation of favorable terms for the permanent financing of the project.

Landowners selling to developers also frequently become equity participants in joint venture activities. The landowner typically contributes land to the project in return for a proportionate ownership interest in the project.

All of the forms of business organization discussed in Chapter Four can be used for joint venture agreements, but the general partnership is the most common. In this arrangement, the developer usually becomes the general partner and is responsible for day-to-day management of the project. The equity investors become limited partners and often have relatively little management involvement in the project. However, the roles played by the parties can vary considerably.

In any joint venture, the roles of the various parties have to be negotiated, and should be carefully spelled out in the partnership agreement. In some cases the equity investors may wish to exercise more control over the project, and may even take the role of general partner. The degree of control desired by the equity investors is affected by such factors as their level of confidence in the developer and his/her track record, the perceived risk involved in the project, the amount of equity contribution required, and the level of the developer's commitment to the project—including whether the developer has made a capital contribution to the project.

There are other significant issues that should be discussed by the prospective partners prior to entering into a joint venture agreement. It is important that the goals of the various partners be similar or complementary. For example, a poorly structured agreement that does not acknowledge the possible interest of one partner in the long-term appreciation of the project, and another's in the cash flow, may result in conflicting desires concerning project management. The prospective partners must also clearly understand the degree of risk each is willing to accept.

The partnership agreement itself should cover certain crucial issues. Of obvious importance is the amount of capital to be contributed, by whom, and when. The agreement must also spell out the return to each of the partners, including any preferred return, as well as the distribution of the cash flow, tax benefits, and reversion. The distribution of responsibility for any losses must also be covered. Related to this issue is the inclusion of a method for raising additional capital, should it be required. A dispute-settling method should also be specified, as well as provisions for withdrawal or death of a partner.

It is the developer's responsibility to provide the prospective joint venture partner with complete information regarding the proposed project. This generally includes site plans, architectural drawings and building specifications, sources and uses of funds required for the project, and financial statements and resumes for the principals. It is the ongoing responsibility of the developer to provide the joint venture partners with current progress reports, including regularly updated cash flow projections.

In summary, a joint venture agreement is a commonly used, practical way to secure the equity necessary for a project. However, it is a complex and variable arrangement requiring detailed and careful consideration to assure that the interests of all the parties are served and protected. Competent legal and financial advice should be sought before entering into a joint venture agreement.

Syndications

Syndications are a second common source of equity for real estate development. While they are most commonly used in residential projects involving rental units, they are such a prominent topic in the real estate industry that they will be discussed here briefly.

By definition, a syndication involves the selling of ownership shares in a project in order to raise cash to acquire land and develop the project. The syndication may involve a large number of investors, each of whom makes only a small equity contribution, or a small group of investors making more significant individual contributions.

Developers may arrange syndications themselves, but they usually turn to professional syndicators when large amounts of capital are needed. When arranging a syndication, a developer may draw on his/her own contacts and those of others involved in the project. The developer must carefully spell out the amount of capital required, the risks involved, and the benefits (including tax benefits). Expert legal and accounting advice is required.

When negotiating a deal with a syndicator, the developer needs to understand how the syndication business works. An agreement with a syndicator can be structured in one of two ways. The syndicator may act as a middleman, who simply markets the ownership shares to prospective investors. Alternatively, the syndicator may actually purchase the ownership shares from the developer and resell them.

The option selected has significant implications for the developer. In the first case, the developer often remains the general partner in the project. In the second case, the syndicator becomes the general partner and the developer remains to provide expertise on a fee basis.

There are advantages and disadvantages to each arrangement. From the developer's perspective, the trade-off is between liability and control. If the developer remains the general partner, he/she retains the principal decision-making position. However, as general partner, the developer has unlimited liability. Conversely, if the syndicator becomes the general partner, the developer loses control over the project. However, he/she will receive a guaranteed fee and incurs no liability.

Syndication involves two major documents. The first is the agreement between the developer and the syndicator. This is referred to as the partnership agreement if the syndicator is playing the middleman role (merely marketing the ownership shares). It is referred to as the purchase agreement if the syndicator is actually purchasing the shares from the developer. In either case the agreement should spell out all aspects of the ownership arrangement, capital contributions, roles of partners, and distribution of risks and benefits.

The second document is the offering memorandum, which is used to market the investment to prospective investors.

The syndicator's compensation is in the form of a percentage of the gross proceeds from the sale of the ownership shares. The syndicator's fee depends on the amount of money to be raised, the time frame during which the money is to be raised, and the type of project.

The syndicator will determine the amount of equity to be raised. The developer must remember that the amount of equity that can be raised is related to the projected financial benefits for the equity investors. It is not determined by the value of the project. The developer must consider whether the amount of money that can be raised can meet the capital requirements of the project, with enough funds remaining to provide him/her with a reasonable profit.

If the developer is to remain the general partner, the amount of risk the developer is willing to assume will have a direct bearing on the ease with which money can be raised, as well as on the amount of money that can be raised. The more risk assumed by the developer—usually in the form of guarantees—the less risk to the equity investors, and the more attractive the investment. A certain minimum guarantee is nearly always required. This may include responsibility for operating deficits, construction cost overruns, and the like. The distribution of risk is a negotiable issue.

Syndications can be the sole source of financing, or they can be combined with debt financing. If debt financing is sought, the involvement of a reputable syndicator can increase the project's attractiveness to lenders, resulting in a more attractive loan package.

The capital contributions solicited through syndication may be made in a single payment, or in installments over time. If the payments are made in installments, the timing of the payments must be negotiated. The payment schedule can be established to coincide with the timing of various expenditures by the developer, such as the purchase of an option on the land, purchase of the land, or actual start of construction.

In summary, syndications are not often used in non-rental residential projects, but are a major source of equity for many real estate projects. They should be considered if the project under consideration can be structured to appeal to investors.

Footnotes

1. Wiedemer, John, *Real Estate Finance*, 3rd Edition, Reston Publishing Co., Reston, Va., 1982.

2. Arnold, Alvin L., *Real Estate Investor's Desk Book*, Warren, Gorham & Lamont, Boston, 1982, p. 6-61.

3. *Ibid*, p. 8-3.

4. Beaton, William R., *Real Estate Finance*, Prentice-Hall Inc., Englewood Cliffs, N.J., 1982, p. 236.

5. *Ibid*, p. 237.

6. *Ibid*, p. 235.

7. Arnold, p. 6-64.

8. Garrett, Joseph, "How Home Builders Use Conventional Forward Take-Out Commitments," *Real Estate Review*, p. 73.

9. *Ibid*, p. 75.

10. Arnold, p. 6-75.

11. In the case of *United States v. Frank Lyon Co.*, 435 U.S. 561 (1978), the U.S. Supreme Court set forth the criteria that should be used in judging the economic realities of a sale/leaseback transaction for purposes of determining whether it would be recognized for tax purposes. The Court attempts to define an objective test that can be applied to any situation as opposed to looking at the subjective intent of the parties, which had been the basis for analysis in most previous cases. The Supreme Court's opinion makes it clear that in evaluating the substance of a sale and leaseback transaction, one very important fact will be whether the transaction involves only two parties. In the Court's view, the presence of a third party assures the independence and arm's length nature of the transaction.

    Another important aspect of the transaction stressed by the Supreme Court in the *Lyon* case was Lyon's personal liability for the mortgage. The Court found that Lyon was weakening his credit position by entering into the transaction. The Court cited the accounting treatment as being significant and stressed that that accounting treatment was consistent with all the parties and in accordance with accepted accounting principles at the time of the transaction. The Supreme Court also cited that Lyon had not been effectively guaranteed a return on its equity investment in the property. Lyon would receive a return only if certain purchase options were exercised and Lyon was taking the financial risk of procuring sufficient rentals of the building during the last 10 years of the ground lease in order to fully realize its return.

    The Supreme Court also took note of the fact that the Internal Revenue Service was unlikely to lose taxes as a result of the way the transaction was structured. No deduction was created by the arrangements, and the transaction had economic viability on its own merits. The transaction was not dependent upon unusual tax arrangements for its practical justification.

12. In the case of *Belz Investment Co. v. Commissioner*, 72 Tax Court 1209 (1979), the Tax Court cited the *Lyon* case and found that a sale/leaseback transaction involving a motel property was legitimate. While the transaction closely resembled a financing arrangement, the Tax Court emphasized the lack of tax avoidance as a factor and pointed to the circumstances beyond the control of the parties that dictated use of the sale/leaseback approach.

In the case of *Hilton v. Commissioner*, 74 Tax Court 305 (1980), the Tax Court found that the sale and leaseback of a department store constituted a financing technique and not a true sale and leaseback. The Court pointed to the fact that rental payments during the 30-year term were calculated to provide the lender with sufficient money to meet the debt service, but no real profit. The investor's potential for gain upon sale of the property was limited, and the likely residual value at the expiration of the lease was minimal. The Court found that only in the event of a condemnation did the investors have the possibility of a substantial economic gain outside of the beneficial tax consequences that they enjoyed. The Tax Court also noted that the paperwork involved in the transaction was sloppy and without sufficient attention to the details of the deal.

The Tax Court again looked at a sale/leaseback transaction involving real estate in the case of *Dunlap v. Commissioner*, 74 Tax Court 104 (1980). This particular transaction involved a standard sale and leaseback deal used by Safeway Stores, Inc., a grocery store chain, to finance the construction of warehouse and distribution space. Although in many ways similar to the Hilton transaction, the sale and leaseback involved in Dunlap was different in several significant respects, and the Tax Court sustained its validity. Investor funds were used to acquire the property and the property involved had substantial potential for appreciation. Safeway had no repurchase option and the investors would have substantial cash flow during the renewal periods during the lease term.

The Fourth Circuit has recently looked very carefully at a sale/leaseback situation involving computer equipment in the case of *Rice Toyota World, Inc. v. Commissioner* 752 F.2d 89 (4th Cir., 1985). The taxpayer entered into an agreement with an unrelated party to purchase and leaseback used computer equipment. The Court found that there was little, if any, likelihood that the taxpayer would ever realize a profit from the transaction and that the only feature of benefit to the taxpayer was the substantial tax benefit to be realized over the lease term.

In the *Rice* case, the Court held that the taxpayer failed to establish that it entered the transaction with a sufficient business purpose and that the transaction was "supported by economic substance." The Court disallowed the deductions on the basis that the transaction lacked economic substance as required in the *Lyon* case. However, the Tax Court in the case of *Estate of Thomas v. Commissioner*, 84 Tax Court 32 (1985), finds economic substance in a computer purchase and leasing transaction that was put together and placed by E.F. Hutton. The Court found that the opinions by Hutton as to residual value were reasonable and that the economics of the situation were viable. The Court found that the lessor reasonably expected a residual value and obtained a reasonable rent during the term of the lease.

General References

Howell, Joseph T., *Real Estate Development Syndication*, Praeger Publishers, New York, 1983.

Maisel, Sherman J., *Financing Real Estate: Principles and Practices*, McGraw-Hill Book Company, New York, 1970.

Land Development 2, National Association of Home Builders, Washington, D.C., 1981.

Chapter Seven
Public Financing Alternatives

Revenue Bonds

Tax-exempt financing for housing development usually involves the issuance of bonds. Mortgage Revenue Bonds (MRBs) are tax-exempt bonds (or comparable financing instruments) that are sold by a governmental or quasi-governmental entity (such as a public housing authority). MRBs can be sold to the general public as securities ("public sale"), or sold as bonds or other debt instruments to institutional buyers such as financial institutions, insurance companies, or pension funds ("private sale").

Proceeds from the sale of MRBs are used to purchase mortgages made to individual home buyers. Industrial Development Bonds or Industrial Revenue Bonds (IRBs) are issued and sold in the same general manner as MRBs and the bond proceeds then are used to fund permanent financing, in the form of a first mortgage, for multifamily rental projects. Both MRBs and IRBs share a common financing principle: only the revenues generated by individual home mortgages (in the case of MRBs) and only the rental revenues generated by the multifamily rental projects (in the case of IRBs) are pledged as security for the tax-exempt bonds or financing instrument. The full faith and credit of the governmental entity issuing the bonds or notes is *not* pledged as security for the bonds, and there is no recourse for bond purchasers against the issuer for any other funds or assets of the issuer in the event of a deficiency or default. Since 1980, both MRBs and IRBs have been subjected to increasing government regulation as a result of the passage of the Mortgage Subsidy Bond Tax Act of 1980,[1] subsequent amendments to the Internal Revenue Code, and the Tax Reform Act of 1986.

Tax-Exempt Financing for Single-Family Housing

In every state except Kansas, state housing finance agencies issue numerous MRBs every year. Many cities and other local governments have their own housing finance agencies, which also issue MRBs. Other municipalities issue tax-exempt bonds for housing through local redevelopment commissions, housing authorities, and other governmental or quasi-governmental agencies or corporations.

Once a viable issuer with legal authority to issue MRBs has been identified, it then must be determined whether that issuer has sufficient bond authority to issue the amount of bonds necessary for the project's financing. The Mortgage Subsidy Bond Tax Act imposed an annual ceiling on the aggregate amount of MRBs issued within any state by the state housing finance agency and local issuers.[2]

The Tax Reform Act of 1986 placed all private activity bonds—that is, bonds not for direct financing of government and certain non-profit organization projects—under a new unified annual state private bond volume limitation. Both MRBs and IRBs for multifamily housing fall within this new volume limitation.[3]

Other federal requirements affecting MRB issuance include:

First-Time Home Buyer Requirement. Eligible recipients of loans funded with the proceeds of MRBs must be "first-time home buyers." The federal definition of a "first-time home buyer" is a person who has not possessed a present ownership interest in his or her principal residence *within three years prior* to the date of closing for the loan financed with MRB proceeds.

Purchase Price Restrictions. The "acquisition cost" of the home to be purchased—meaning the cost of acquiring a completed unit from a seller—must not exceed 90 percent of the average area purchase price for housing in the area in which the unit is located.[3] The U.S. Treasury Department periodically publishes average area purchase price information for both new construction and existing housing stock, for each of the states, and for particular areas within the states known as Standard Metropolitan Statistical Areas (SMSAs).[4]

Principal Residence Requirement. The unit to be financed must be intended for use by the borrower as his/her principal residence.[3] This requirement usually is satisfied by presenting a sworn affidavit at closing, which states that the borrower intends to occupy the residence within 60 days following the closing and that the home being financed with the MRB proceeds will be the borrower's principal residence. Obviously this requirement is intended to preclude investor purchases and to ensure that this type of financing will be used for owner-occupied buildings only.

Federal requirements for MRBs also contain exceptions to these three requirements for areas within cities that were designated as "targeted areas" by the Mortgage Subsidy Bond Act and the Tax Reform Act of 1986. Generally, an MRB issue can maintain its tax-exempt status as long as 95 percent of the loans financed with the proceeds of the MRB issue comply with the three basic requirements outlined above.[3] For homes located in the targeted areas, the first-time home buyer requirement does not apply, and the maximum purchase price is limited to 110 percent of the average area purchase price. Initially, at least 20 percent of every MRB issue must be reserved for loans to finance residences located in any targeted areas within the territorial jurisdiction of the lender.[3]

Targeted areas generally are defined as specific census tracts identified by the Treasury Department as depressed areas with inadequate housing stock.[3] Generally, the targeted areas initially identified by the Treasury were severely depressed areas located within urban centers, many of which were primarily industrial in character and had virtually no housing stock, and/or little property with development potential. Federal regulations allow cities to use an alternate mechanism for defining targeted areas, where the cities define "areas of chronic economic distress" (ACEDs), which are then certified by the state government, and sent to the U.S. Department of Housing and Urban Development (HUD) for final approval. HUD notifies the Treasury Department of all designated ACED areas, which are treated as targeted areas for the purpose of financing regulations.

Federal restrictions on MRBs contain a 20 percent low- and moderate-income requirement, but no upper income limits. However, virtually every state housing finance agency (HFA) is limited through state legislation to serving only lower- and moderate-income persons and families. MRBs issued by state and local housing finance agencies generally are limited to persons having an annual income less than or equal to the maximum moderate income limit established and published by the agency. However, some local issuers are not subject to the same moderate income limits that apply to the state HFAs. In some cases local issuers have no income limits whatsoever, so that the income for eligible borrowers is limited only by the federal maximum purchase price and the resulting market restraints.

Many cities and developers have developed innovative approaches to MRB financing by applying for ACED designation for an existing project site or urban redevelopment area. As a result of the special treatment afforded to targeted areas, mortgages funded by MRBs for residences located in targeted areas can be used to finance more expensive homes, as long as the home is the buyer's principal residence. The first-time home buyer requirement does not apply to MRBs in targeted areas, and the maximum allowable purchase price is larger than for homes in non-targeted areas funded by MRBs.

Industrial Revenue Bonds for Multifamily Housing

Federal Requirements

Industrial revenue bonds for housing are among a broad variety of tax-exempt revenue bonds issued by state and local governments for a variety of purposes, such as sports facilities, wharves and docks, industrial development, and pollution control facilities. As a result of perceived abuses in the field of industrial revenue bond issuance (the financing of shopping centers and fast-food restaurants have been cited frequently as examples of abuses), Congress has imposed significant constraints on state and local government issuance of IRBs. Prior to the Tax Reform Act of 1986, each state had an annual aggregate limit on the total amount of outstanding industrial revenue bonds that it could issue, and IRBs for housing were exempt from the annual IRB issuance limit. MRBs for housing are no longer exempt from the annual volume limitation.[3]

IRBs for multifamily housing were traditionally used only in conjunction with Section 8-type rental subsidy programs. For example, many housing authorities are authorized by state law to issue only federally insured bonds pursuant to Section 11(b) of the National Housing Act for projects receiving rental subsidy payments. With the decline and fall of Section 8 and other related federal subsidy programs, state and local issuers now enter into bond financing programs to facilitate multifamily rental projects that do not receive rental subsidies.

Until the end of 1985, federal laws and regulations required projects financed with the proceeds of a tax-exempt IRB for housing to reserve 20 percent (15 percent in targeted areas) of the units in the project for persons of low or moderate income. The definition of "low or moderate income" for this purpose was a person or family, regardless of size, with an income less than 80 percent of the area median income.[5] This definition was changed by the Tax Reform Act of 1986. The new targeting requirement specifies that at least 20 percent of the units must be set aside for families earning 50 percent or less of area median income, or, alternatively, at least 40 percent of the units must be set aside for families earning 60 percent or less of area median income; in both cases adjusted for family size.[6]

Multifamily rental projects financed with the proceeds of an IRB for housing must be maintained as rental projects (condominium conversions or resales for non-rental purposes are not permitted) for 10 years after 50 percent occupancy has been achieved, or until one-half the term of the bond maturity has been reached, or until the date that any Section 8 rental assistance involved in the project terminates.[7] Amendments to the tax code applicable to IRBs for housing, which can be found in the Tax Equalization and Financial Responsibility Act of 1982, require the issuer to conduct a public hearing on each multifamily project to be financed with IRBs.

Eligible Issuers

As with MRBs, identification of an appropriate IRB issuer is extremely important. Most housing finance agencies participate in multifamily bond issues, which will be discussed in detail in the next section. Various local issuers have also been given adequate statutory authority to enter into multifamily IRB financings.

Mortgage Insurance

IRBs for housing traditionally have been issued for projects accepted for FHA mortgage issuance under Section 221(d)(4), USC, and issuers generally regard FHA insurance as excellent security for bond issuance. Recent innovations in multifamily bond financing include the financing of projects insured with private mortgage insurance, usually in conjunction with some form of surety arrangement for the bond issue (that is, insurance of the repayment of bonds by a rated commercial bank or insurance company), or the use of some form of credit enhancement. Recently, FHA has proposed to extend 221(d)(4) insurance—which in the past has been available only for fixed-rate, fully amortized loans—to other types of mortgage instruments, including Partially Amortizing Mortgages (PAMs), Call Provision Mortgages (CPMs) and Graduated Payment Mortgages (GPMs).

Improvement of Multifamily Project Market Feasibility

In the current multifamily housing development market, the financial feasibility "window" for unsubsidized projects subject to the federal occupancy income restrictions is marginal at best, even with below-market interest rates for permanent financing. To improve the financial feasibility of the projects, some innovative underwriters of multifamily issues use nontraditional financing instruments—most involving enhancement of the creditworthiness and financial vitality of the project—as a basis for adjusting the resulting bond rating and interest rate on the IRBs issued to finance the project. Credit enhancement techniques that have been used successfully in the bond market in recent months include: Section 223(f) USC Co-insurance; the Federal National Mortgage Association (Fannie Mae)

Tax-Exempt Financing PLUS Program; the Municipal Bond Insurance Association (MBIA) Direct Real Estate Guarantee Program; the Guaranteed Payment Loan to Developer Program (GIC); a surety or guaranty-type program involving irrevocable letters of credit; guaranteed investment contracts and a surety bond or other guaranty instrument; and various letter-of-credit arrangements.

Each of these programs involves close coordination of the particular financial requirements of a project with the bond underwriter involved in structuring the bond issue.[8] Of paramount importance to the multifamily developer is, of course, the ultimate cost of the mortgage. Each of the credit enhancement techniques outlined above involves fees in addition to the underwriters' fees, the bond counsel fees, trustees' fees, if any, and other costs of bond issuance. As a general rule, the total of fees and costs for a multipurpose bond transaction might range between three percent and four-and-a-half percent of the face amount of the bond issue.

Restrictions contained in the Tax Reform Act of 1986 involving allowable recovery of the costs of bond issuance have made taxable bonds an attractive alternative.

Summary

In the rapidly changing housing market, many factors shape the eventual structure of any financing involving tax-exempt bonds. The state of the art of housing bond financing is still measured in terms of flexibility, and new financial instruments are continually evolving to meet specific project needs.

Housing Finance Agencies

State and local housing finance agencies traditionally have served as a source of single-family mortgages, placing several hundred million dollars worth of loans each year. In addition to funding single-family mortgages for low- and moderate-income persons through the issuance of MRBs, housing finance agencies finance hundreds of multifamily projects by providing below-market interest rate development loans for sponsors of multifamily projects that serve lower- and moderate-income tenants and buyers.

Single-Family Programs

As discussed at the beginning of this chapter, housing finance agencies issue MRBs at a tax-exempt bond rate, and then add the cost of issuance, and a portion of operating expenses as an additional interest rate spread. The combination of the agency's spread and the tax-exempt bond rate yields a below-market mortgage interest rate for the home buyer.

Although some housing finance agencies may service loans themselves, most work through a mortgage purchase program. The HFA contracts with a servicing lender or lenders to originate and process the loan packages, send the completed loan package to the agency for approval, and then make the actual mortgage loan to the home buyer. The loan eventually is purchased by the agency.

The state or local housing finance agency sizes bond issues by estimating the future mortgage demand, but has to stay within the applicable annual state ceiling that limits mortgage revenue bond issuance. Factors considered when estimating future statewide mortgage demand are: surveys of the housing market; the existing statewide demand for below-market mortgages; the demand for such mortgages by lenders willing to participate in the HFA's mortgage purchase program; and the demonstrated demand from builders for below-market-rate financing for units under development that meet the federal purchase price restrictions.

The current bond market and resulting tax-exempt interest rates are also taken into consideration when structuring a bond issue. The traditional approach to delivery of the tax-exempt bond proceeds for purchase of mortgage loans has been on a lender commitment basis. In a lender commitment program, the housing finance agency surveys demand by lenders throughout its jurisdiction and contracts with individual lenders to purchase mortgages in an aggregate amount representing a mortgage purchase commitment to a particular lender. Thereafter, the lender, either on a first-come, first-served basis or on a lottery basis, accepts applications from individual borrowers who qualify for the loan and meet the federal restrictions on MRBs (the first-time home buyer, maximum purchase price, and principal residence requirements). Approved loans are purchased by the agency with the proceeds of the HFA's single-family bond issue.

The second mechanism for delivering bond proceeds to purchase individual mortgage loans is through a system of builder commitments. In a builder commitment program, proceeds of an entire bond issue, or a portion of a particular bond issue, are earmarked for commitments to particular builders who have indicated a demand for below market-rate mortgage loan financing as permanent financing for units that are planned or under construction.

The state or local housing finance agency surveys builders throughout its service area to determine initial demand. Then the agency sizes a bond issue, or creates a reservation within a larger bond issue, for builder commitments. Builders then enter into commitment agreements with the agency—using a local lender as a conduit, originator, and servicer—to purchase mortgage loans in an aggregate amount at a specified maximum interest rate. The participating builder pays a commitment fee, generally nonrefundable, that is a percentage or fractional percentage of the aggregate amount of the mortgage loans committed to the individual builder. The builder is then given a specified period of time—usually about one year—during which to complete or build units within the maximum purchase price restrictions for that geographic area, and to locate and qualify applicants for the mortgage loans committed to the builder. Often, extensions of the commitment period are available for a fee from the housing finance agency.

As a result of the phasing out of the Section 8 program and other rental assistance programs funded by the federal government, housing finance agencies are exploring various mechanisms for providing additional single-family mortgage loan assistance to persons qualifying for tax-exempt financing. One program currently in operation provides monthly mortgage payment subsidies to selected, very low-income home buyers receiving mortgage loans funded with bond proceeds.[9] These subsidies are used to buy down the borrower's monthly mortgage payments in exchange for a second mortgage on the property being financed with the housing finance agency's first mortgage loan. Subsidy payments, secured in the form of a second mortgage, are not repaid until the residence is resold by the subsidy recipient. The housing finance agency is repaid only from appreciation, if any, of the value of the property during the time between first purchase and resale.

Other programs are under consideration to provide additional state and local government sources of funding. These programs would either subsidize monthly mortgage payments, or provide funds to buy down the tax-exempt interest rates of mortgage loans offered as a result of housing finance agency bond issues.

Multifamily Programs

Housing finance agencies usually offer multifamily project financing through two bond issuance techniques. Agencies will often schedule two or three bond issues annually, grouping several eligible projects into each bond issue. For FHA insured projects, approval for FHA insurance (initial endorsement) is generally required prior to issuance and sale of the bonds. In some states this can result in extreme timing pressures for the developer, since FHA processing time nationwide averages four to five months, and in some area offices is even longer.

An alternate method used by some housing finance agencies allows the agency to undertake single-family project bond issues. Generally, the cost of bond issuance on a per project basis can be substantially higher when a separate bond issue is used for each project, although these additional costs may be outweighed by the costs incurred due to time delays while waiting for the next grouped project bond issue.[10]

Housing finance agencies, like other lenders, are searching for new methods of providing effective mortgage instruments with the lowest possible interest rates for developers of multifamily low- and moderate-income rental housing, who have been hard-hit by repeal of rent subsidy programs. Some housing finance agencies are considering, or experimenting with, rental subsidy programs in which a portion of the monthly rent of some of the lower- and moderate-income tenants is offset by a direct rental subsidy payment from the state housing finance agency. This technique can be used by the state agency to make rental housing affordable for persons with incomes even lower than the usual income profile for qualifying tenants.

Another area of new interest and activity for state housing finance agencies is the financing of congregate care facilities for elderly persons. HUD now approves 221(d)(4) USC insurance for these facilities, and has provided guidelines for congregate care facilities eligible for HUD mortgage interest coverage.[11]

Congregate care facilities are not rest homes. They are a hybrid form of group living for elderly persons where the monthly payment covers rental of the dwelling unit, plus maintenance and operating costs for onsite recreational and social facilities, and a full-time food service operation.

While a nurse or comparably trained health staff person is provided onsite, congregate care facilities do not offer the skilled nursing attention provided in a nursing home or rest home.

Housing Rehabilitation and Home Improvement Programs

While single-family MRBs and multifamily IRBs have been discussed solely within the context of new construction, financing is also available for rehabilitation of existing owner-occupied single-family housing, and, under appropriate circumstances, for the rehabilitation and refinancing of eligible multifamily projects.

Many housing finance agencies also have entered into home improvement loan programs. Such programs provide low-interest second mortgage loans for basic renovation of older or deteriorating owner-occupied housing units—including insulation, weatherproofing, heating, air conditioning, electrical and plumbing modernization.

At least one state agency has entered into agreements with local governments to make use of local government allocations of Community Development Block Grant (CDBG) funds from HUD to provide seed money for home improvement bond issues. Under this concept, CDBG money is included as an additional cash reserve by local governments in order to produce the lowest possible bond interest rate. Using this approach, second mortgage home improvement loans with interest rates as low as 4 or 5 percent can be generated.

Future of Housing Finance Agencies

The Tax Reform Act of 1986 affected the operation of state housing finance agencies and other tax-exempt issuers. The law contains significant restrictions on the issuance of tax-exempt bonds, and an MRB sunset date. The state private activity bond limitations set forth in the 1986 tax act dramatically affect the level of housing bond issuance activity in many states. Issuers in the tax-exempt housing bond market will continue to seek alternative financing techniques, including taxable bonds, and hopefully will continue to provide below-market interest rate permanent financing for single-family mortgages and multifamily housing development loans.

Tax Increment Financing

Tax increment financing (TIF) is an unusual and powerful public sector financing tool for certain types of projects. TIF programs work best in connection with larger, mixed-use projects that involve commercial facilities. Commercial uses are important because they have the potential to generate sales tax revenue. Under certain TIF statutes, that revenue, along with increased real estate taxes, may constitute a source of funds to either secure the bonds issued as part of the TIF program or to defray certain costs subsidized by a municipality in connection with a TIF program.

TIF programs typically focus on the allocation of taxes already collected, and do not affect tax payments, or involve grants or loans from the general funds of the municipality. Under TIF programs, the taxes generated by a particular project are used to defray certain costs incurred in connection with that project. TIF programs appeal to developers because the increment of taxes generated by their projects constitute an additional source of funds that are not typically available to developers. This increment becomes available to help pay for certain project costs.

The operation of a TIF program is best illustrated by an example. Suppose a developer contemplates a mixed-use project—including office, residential, hotel, and retail facilities. Assume the site is vacant, and generates very little real estate tax revenue or other tax revenue for the municipality in which it is located. After the property is improved, it will be subject to reassessment for real estate tax purposes, and the retail sales made there will also generate tax revenue. The municipality and the developer thus can estimate the incremental tax revenue increase to be generated as a result of the development. That amount can be used to secure the payment of bonds issued to defray certain development costs, or to pay those costs directly. In either case the costs must be permissible under the relevant TIF statute. The TIF program in effect in Illinois is described below. For comparison and reference purposes, descriptions of the TIF programs in Indiana, Minnesota, Ohio, California, and Florida are included in Appendix 7-A.

TIF programs have become more widespread in recent years. As of 1981, one author reported that 26 states had enacted TIF programs.[12] Just two years earlier, an article in *Urban Law Review* indicated only 14 states had TIF programs.[13]

TIF programs are aimed primarily at the redevelopment of blighted neighborhoods and are based on the assumption that redevelopment will increase property values in the redevelopment area. The increase in property values, the assumption continues, leads to the "increment" component of Tax Increment Financing.

Simply put, this "increment" in revenues is the difference between the municipality's income from property and sales taxes in the blighted area prior to redevelopment, as well as the municipality's revenues after redevelopment. As one court aptly observed:

> The basic purpose of statutes authorizing the creation of tax incremental districts is to enable the increased tax revenues generated by community redevelopment projects to be placed in a special fund for the purpose of repaying the public costs of the projects.[14]

TIF statutes generally provide that this increment can be used in two ways. It can pay directly for improvements to be constructed in connection with the redevelopment area. Alternatively, it can be pledged to the retirement of bonds issued by the municipality at the outset of the redevelopment program to generate funds to pay for certain costs associated with the development. The statute in Illinois specifies those costs for which a municipality may choose to assume responsibility. Under either the direct payment or the bond approach, however, the municipality will assume responsibility for certain costs that a developer may otherwise have to bear.

Representative Statute

Illinois

Tax increment financing is authorized in Illinois by a statute that allows municipalities and developers to work together to improve certain "blighted property," or "conservation areas," or "industrial park conservation areas."[15]

The municipality benefits from the development or redevelopment of property within its taxing jurisdiction and from other advantageous consequences of development. As in other states, the developer benefits under the Illinois law, because the municipality allocates the increase in property taxes resulting from the development or redevelopment to costs incurred by the municipality and the developer.

Under the statute, the municipality may take responsibility for certain costs associated with the development, including:

- Costs of studies and surveys, plans and specifications, and professional service costs including, but not limited to, architectural, engineering, legal, marketing, financial, planning and special services
- Property assembly costs, including the acquisition of land and other property, real or personal, demolition of buildings and the clearing and grading of land
- Costs of construction of public works or improvements
- Financing costs stemming from the issuance of the obligations issued under the TIF program[16]

Moreover, the municipality is given the power to acquire by purchase, donation, lease, or eminent domain any property within a redevelopment area. The costs that a municipality chooses to incur can be funded either from the general budget or through the issuance of bonds. As discussed below, the maturity period of the bonds used cannot exceed 20 years.

To use TIF, a municipality must enact two ordinances: one that approves the redevelopment plan and the specific projects, and designates a redevelopment area; and one specifically approving the use of TIFs in conjunction with the redevelopment area.

There are certain substantive and procedural prerequisites that must be satisfied. Most important of the substantive prerequisites is the qualification of the property (the "redevelopment area") as either a "blighted area" or a "conservation area." A conservation area is defined under the statute as an area in which at least 50 percent of the structures are 35 years or older, and which contains at least three of the factors necessary to qualify as an improved blighted area (see below).[17]

The definition of a "blighted area" includes two subcategories: "vacant" and "improved." The statute specifies the elements that must be present before a parcel may qualify under either subcategory. Vacant land is defined as follows:

> [A]ny parcel or combination of parcels of real property without industrial, commercial or residential buildings which has not been used for commercial agricultural purposes within five years prior to the designation of the redevelopment project area, unless such parcel has been subdivided. The changes in the definition of vacant land made by this amendatory Act of 1984 shall apply to taxing districts containing such land created on or after June 30, 1984.[18]

To be deemed blighted, vacant land must contain at least two of the following four factors:

- Obsolete platting of the vacant land
- Diversity of ownership of such vacant land
- Tax and special assessment delinquencies on such land
- Deterioration of structures or site improvements in areas adjacent to the vacant land

Vacant property may also be characterized as blighted if the area would have qualified as a blighted area immediately prior to becoming vacant. Areas will qualify as blighted if they contain quarries or railyards, rail tracks or railroad rights-of-way.[19]

Alternatively, "improved land" will be considered blighted if the improvements are detrimental to public safety, health, morals or welfare. The statute presumes that existing improvements are detrimental if any five or more of the following fourteen factors are present: age; dilapidation; obsolescence; deterioration; illegal use of individual structures; presence of structures below minimum code standards; excessive vacancies; overcrowding of structures and community facilities; lack of ventilation, light or sanitary facilities; inadequate utilities; excessive land coverage; deleterious land use or layout; depreciation of physical maintenance; or lack of community planning.

Industrial park conservation areas are also eligible for TIF programs. An industrial park conservation area is an area within a labor surplus municipality—or within 1½ miles of its corporate limits in some cases—where there is vacant land suitable for an industrial park.

By definition, labor surplus municipalities have unemployment rates in excess of 6 percent and equal to at least 100 percent of the average national unemployment rates released by the U.S. Labor Department within the six-month period preceding the date the municipality designates the redevelopment area.

In addition to requirements regarding the condition of the property, the statute requires the municipality to make certain determinations regarding the development and imposes substantive requirements on redevelopment plans. The municipality must conclude:

- That the proposed site has not been subject to growth and development through investment by private enterprise and would not reasonably be anticipated to be developed without the adoption of the redevelopment plan
- That the redevelopment plan and project conforms to the comprehensive plan for the development of the municipality as a whole; and
- The redevelopment plan must state estimated dates (which shall not be more than 23 years from the adoption of the ordinance approving the redevelopment area) of completion of the redevelopment project and retirement of obligations incurred to finance redevelopment project costs

The first substantive test—the absence of private development—is the most crucial. The developer must be able to demonstrate that *but for* the TIF assistance, the project would not be completed. In addition, in an industrial park conservation area, the municipality in question must be a labor surplus municipality.

Once a municipality has passed these threshold tests, certain procedural steps must be followed. The first step is the preparation of a redevelopment plan and the submission of that plan to the municipality or one of its commissions. The redevelopment plan must explain how the program will accomplish the desired objectives, and must include:

- Estimated redevelopment project costs
- Sources of funds to pay such costs
- Nature and term of obligations to be issued
- Most recent equalized assessed valuation of the Redevelopment Project Area
  Estimate of the equalized assessed valuation after redevelopment; and
- General land uses to apply in the proposed redevelopment project area

In the event of an industrial park conservation area, the redevelopment plan must also include:

- Description of any proposed developer, user, and tenant of any of the property in the redevelopment project area
- A description of the type, structure, and general character of the facilities the developer contemplates for the redevelopment project area
- A description of the type, class, and number of employees to be employed in the operation of these facilities; and
- The terms of the annexation agreement if the redevelopment project area is to be annexed

Next, the municipality is required to hold public hearings to consider the designation of a redevelopment project area. In connection with such a hearing, the municipality must comply with the stringent notice requirements set forth in the statute. At the hearing, any interested person or affected taxing district may file written objections with the clerk and can make an oral statement.

Significantly, some of the most vehement opposition may arise from other taxing districts that, but for the TIF program's use of the increase in tax revenues, would enjoy the benefits stemming from the redevelopment. The argument often used to still these complaints is that *but for* the TIF program there would be no redevelopment and hence no increased revenues. Thus, according to this argument, the other taxing authorities are in no worse position than if there were no TIF program.

The municipality is given 14 to 90 days to introduce an ordinance approving a redevelopment plan and project, and designating a redevelopment project area. At the time that the redevelopment project area is designated, the municipality may also pass a "TIF ordinance" that provides for the allocation and distribution of incremental taxes arising from the redevelopment project area in each year after the TIF ordinance is passed.

Through the passage of these ordinances, the municipality acquires broad discretionary powers in connection with the TIF program and the redevelopment area. These powers include:

- The power to enter into contracts
- The power to sell, acquire, lease, etc., all property, real or personal, in any manner reasonably necessary for the municipality to achieve the objectives of the plan. Some bidding rules are mandated, including a provision regarding competitive bidding
- The power to create a supervisory commission
- The power to incur project costs and issue obligations secured by the special tax allocation fund to pay these costs. The maturity of the obligations cannot exceed 20 years

No public referendum is required to issue the municipality's obligations unless the municipality secures the obligations by pledging the "full faith and credit of the municipality." Such a pledge entitles the voters to petition for a referendum, and the petition must be filed within 45 days after the publication of the ordinance. The municipality can avoid a public referendum by issuing obligations secured by the net revenues from all or part of the project, any or all property taxes collected by the municipality, or any other taxes or anticipated receipts that the municipality may lawfully pledge.[20]

To implement a TIF program, the city clerk is required to determine the most recent assessed value of each plot and tract within the redevelopment area. The sum of these values is used to determine the Total Initial Equalized Assessed Value of the taxable real property in the development area.[21]

Each year thereafter, the clerk is required to reassess the value of the property. That portion of the property value, up to the Total Initial Equalized Assessed Value, is taxed and distributed to the various taxing districts as if no redevelopment plan were in existence. The portion in excess of the Total Initial Equalized Assessed Value—that is, the portion of the new real estate assessment that is assumed to be attributable to the increase in property values created by the redevelopment project—is placed in a special tax allocation fund. In addition, all funds received by the municipality upon the sale, lease, or disposition of property within the redevelopment area are also placed in the special tax allocation fund. The municipal treasurer then uses this fund to pay project costs and to retire any obligations incurred by the municipality for the project.[22]

In addition to acquiring funds for development from the increased property assessments in the redevelopment area, the municipality that adopts TIF prior to 1987 may, by ordinance, authorize the department of revenue to pay the municipality an amount equal to the increase in the aggregate amount of sales taxes paid by retailers and servicepersons on transactions at places of business located in the redevelopment project area. After 1987, a municipality may also seek to be paid any increase in state and local charges for gas, electric, and telecommunications charged to owners or tenants in the redevelopment area.

Finally, once the obligations of the municipality have been retired, the fund is dissolved; the area ceases to be designated a redevelopment project area; and all taxes are again distributed to the taxing entities as though the TIF plan had never been adopted.[23]

Application of TIF

TIF is best suited for the development of shopping centers, office buildings, hotels, industrial complexes, and other income-generating projects because of its dependence on an increase in property values and the corresponding increase in property and sales tax revenues.

TIF can be used in conjunction with condemnation proceedings to acquire land for redevelopment projects. The municipality purchases land using funds generated by the sale of bonds, which, in turn, are secured by the tax increment. Once the municipality acquires the property, it is conveyed to a developer at an attractive price. The developer acquires a parcel that might not otherwise be possible to assemble, at a lower price than would otherwise be available. The cost of the condemnation proceedings will be covered by the TIF income. It should be noted that the TIF statute in some states does not in itself authorize a municipality to condemn land.[24]

Alternatively, TIF can be used for the improvement of land instead of its acquisition. For example, a shopping center developer might urge a municipality to use the revenue increment to construct access lanes, traffic signals, curb cuts, detention ponds, storm sewers, water lines, and sanitary sewers. The developer is relieved of the cost of these items. Developers must use caution in approaching municipalities with proposals like these, however. If the developer gives the impression that he/she will build the project anyway, but is looking for "sweeteners," the municipality may be precluded from finding that *but for* the TIF program, redevelopment would not occur.

Although TIF has many potential applications, it is most useful for the financing of certain "start-up" costs. TIF is not well suited for long-term financing. Moreover, as some critics have emphasized, TIF is not a strong source of financing for projects that will not generate significant increases in property value. As one author observed: "The incremental value created by low- and moderate-income housing will not pay for the cost of the housing."[25]

TIF statutes have been attacked on a number of grounds, including questions of equal protection and conformity with tax uniformity clauses, improper delegation of a legislative function, and improper lending.

In most states the courts have measured TIF statutes against minimal constitutional tests and found them constitutional.[26] Generally, TIF programs can survive a constitutional challenge as long as the program is *reasonably related* to the public purpose articulated in the enabling statute.

Moreover, the legitimacy of a TIF program will not be invalidated merely because a private party may gain benefit. As long as the private gain is incidental to the public purpose of redevelopment, the TIF program should survive a challenge founded on the benefit flowing to the private developer. Indeed, a court that concludes that a TIF program is reasonably related to a public purpose will likely characterize any private benefit as "incidental."[27]

Similarly, many courts have upheld TIF statutes against arguments that TIF creates a tax system that is neither uniform nor equal. As one court explained, although the *distribution* of collected taxes may not be equal among taxing districts, the rate of property assessment remains uniform and equal as far as the taxpayer is concerned.[28] As we will see in the next section of this chapter covering tax abatement financing, however, this approach has not been applied uniformly by the courts.

Despite what often appears to be a judicial presumption of their validity, TIF programs are not invincible. A Kentucky court struck down an entire program on two grounds: first, that the state legislature could not delegate the designation of development boundaries to local authorities; and second, that the TIF statute violated the state constitutional prohibition on the expenditure of school funds for non-school purposes.[29]

Although no other court has invalidated a TIF statute in its entirety, other state courts have imposed certain limitations. For example, the Iowa Supreme Court concluded that a municipality's use of TIF was subject to the 5 percent debt limitation imposed on local governments.[30]

Moreover, some courts appear willing to entertain challenges to a local determination that an area is blighted. For example, in *Sweetwater Valley Civic Association v. National City,* the California Supreme Court held that a determination by a local government that an area constituted "blight" was incorrect.[31] In this case, a large part of the "blight area" was a golf course. The court disagreed with the municipality's conclusion that the golf course constituted blight and held instead:

> The real property subject to this action has not become an economic liability within the purview of [the Act]; nor is there evidence of "social" blight. Drainage and soil problems—and even condemnation of part of the golf course—while no doubt burdening the property, have not ended its present economic use. To the contrary, the evidence reveals the golf course is at best marginally profitable. While the costs of removing the easements and solving the drainage problems make private redevelopment infeasible, that issue arises only after first finding the subject property is blighted. In the circumstances, the golf course is being economically profitable—in combination with its open space nature—the property therefore constitutes neither an economic nor a social liability. Therefore, it is not blighted.

Similarly, in *Apostle v. City of Seattle,*[33] the Supreme Court of Washington held that the Seattle City Council's bald assertion that an area was blighted was subject to review, and, in the absence of evidence to support the conclusion of "blight," would be overruled. The court remanded the case so that the City Council could articulate the reasons for the "blight" designation.[34]

Even so, it is unlikely that a TIF program will fail as a result of a judicial challenge. Outside of the courts, however, significant questions are being raised about the wisdom of TIF programs. As noted above, the principal assumption underlying TIF programs is *but for* the redevelopment, the blighted area would not experience an increase in tax revenues. One study, however, suggests that much of the increase in tax revenues is unrelated and, in many instances, occurs prior to the redevelopment activities.[35]

Moreover, the TIF programs themselves can be subject to abuse. For example, a municipality may draw the lines of a redevelopment area to capture the increment from development that is likely to occur even without the redevelopment project. This deprives other taxing authorities with jurisdiction over the redevelopment area of their revenue.

The discussion above focuses on TIF programs from a developer's perspective, including the potential uses of TIF funds (and the limits on such uses), the application process, and challenges to such programs. The developer, however, must also be cognizant of those tax concerns that may affect the success of a TIF program. Foremost among such concerns is whether the bonds issued by a municipality in connection with a TIF program will be taxable or tax-exempt. The Tax Reform Act of 1986 suggests that many such bonds will now be taxable.

In general, under the Tax Reform Act of 1986, interest paid on municipal bonds can be tax-exempt only if such bonds are used to finance traditional government activities. Thus if bonds are used for "private" or "nonessential" purposes, the interest will be taxable. While there are exceptions, the Tax Reform Act of 1986 severely limited those instances in which such bonds can be tax-exempt. Additional information on the Act is included in Appendix 7-B.

Summary

Tax increment financing offers the potential developer a source of funds to pay for certain improvements associated with the redevelopment of a blighted or decayed area. For a developer who anticipates large expenditures for land acquisition and/or infrastructure, *and* who can present convincing evidence that the redevelopment will generate significant increases in land values (and the corresponding increase in tax revenues), TIF offers a potentially significant source of funds.

Conversely, TIF programs may be of little practical use to a developer whose plans will not generate significant increases in land values, or to a developer of land that is already assessed at a high value. Still, it is wise for developers to explore the possibility of tax increment financing.

Tax Abatement Financing

In contrast to tax increment financing, tax abatement programs can offer immediate and direct reduction of the amount of tax a property owner must pay. Under a tax abatement program, a taxpayer is relieved of his/her obligation to pay all or part of taxes due on certain property for a specified period of time.

Tax abatement programs can be directed at large groups, or they can be tailored specifically to the needs of a particular developer. Tax abatement programs can be aimed at the general objective of economic revitalization,[36] or at a more specific objective, such as pollution control.[37] Whatever the objective, the underlying concept remains the same: the property owner is encouraged to undertake certain projects because they offer relief from taxes. As one court observed in evaluating a tax abatement program:

> The purpose of [the program] was to encourage the improvement of real property for commercial, business and industrial facilities, including the improvement of obsolete facilities.[38]

Many states have adopted tax abatement programs aimed at large groups of property owners. New York has had such a tax exemption program since 1956. J. Griffith describes the New York City program as follows:[39]

> [The program] induces an owner to improve a multiple dwelling by granting a 12-year tax exemption from any increase in the assessed valuation of the structure resulting from these improvements. The law provides for tax abatements on both the structure and the land upon which it is built. These abatements may be up to 9 percent of the city's determination of [the] reasonable costs of the improvements with a limit of 8⅓ percent of such reasonable cost allowed to be abated in any one year for a period not to exceed 20 years. If in any one year the abatement is greater than the tax due, the Owner's taxes will be reduced to zero.

New York City's program can be used with a variety of residential programs, including the conversion of commercial nonresidential properties into residential properties. Indeed, the author cited above reports that developers have used this program to convert hotels into apartment complexes. Others, however, have argued that the success of New York City's program lies in the fact that, beyond tax abatements, the program actually represents a large-scale subsidy for *rehabilitation*.[40]

The Pennsylvania Department of Commerce describes its tax abatement program as follows:

> The Local Economic Revitalization Tax Assistance Act (LERTA) allows any county, city, borough, incorporated town, township, institution or school district to abate real estate taxes for a period of time not to exceed 10 years. Improvements eligible for this abatement include construction, reconstruction, additions, alterations, or repairs to existing structures. The Tax exemption may be based on actual costs or uniform maximum costs set by the governing body.

In New Jersey, a program labeled the Urban Industrial Parks Program is described as follows:

> Improved sites with public improvements are available for sale at competitive prices. Newly constructed facilities can usually qualify for 15-year property tax abatement.[41]

Many of the tax exemption programs are self-implementing—if a property owner meets certain well defined criteria, his/her taxes will abate. An obvious advantage of a self-implementing program is the ease and relatively low cost of administration.[42] A taxpayer who wants to take advantage of a tax abatement program need only meet certain criteria and apply for the tax exemption. By contrast, use of tax increment financing programs involves public hearings, securing the redevelopment area designation, and assisting in the sale of bonds.

Although they are relatively easy to administer, disputes concerning eligibility for exemptions and the amount of taxes due occur under tax exemption programs.

The *Dorem Corporation v. Government of the Virgin Islands* [43] case illustrates an issue frequently under dispute—whether the applying taxpayer satisfies the statutory criteria for receiving the abatement. In *Dorem Corporation,* the issue was whether a corporation qualified under a tax exemption program that was primarily designed for businesses engaged in the construction or operation of commercial buildings. The court held that the exemption did not apply, reasoning that the building had already been completed prior to the corporation's acquisition of it, and that the corporation was not "in any true sense operating a commercial building."

Another risk is that, under certain circumstances, the benefits of the tax exemption can be revoked. For example, benefits under New York City's Program can be revoked as follows:[44]

> The City revokes benefits if a building in the [tax abatement] program later becomes used for commercial or hotel purposes, or, if real estate taxes or water or sewer charges with respect to [the building] remain unpaid. . .
>
> To prevent a mortgagee from being caught unaware of owner violations, the regulations provide that no revocation shall take place unless the breach or omission remains outstanding following the elapse of 30 days after notice has been given to the owner or mortgagee.

Accordingly, the local developer is advised to determine early in the planning process what conditions may lead to a revocation of the tax exemption.

A legal treatise explains the government's power to grant tax exemptions to a specific group or individual as follows:[45]

> Although there is authority to the contrary, it is now generally held that unless limited from doing so by the local constitution, the state may enter into a binding contract to exempt from taxation, forever or for a definite term, property which in its discretion it could have exempted from taxation by general legislative grants of immunity. The power of the state to tax property in specific instances may be surrendered by one legislative body so as to bind succeeding legislatures. In the absence of special restrictions in its constitution, a state may make a valid contract with a private corporation for its exemption from taxation, complete or partial, for a limited time or in perpetuity.

Note that "the exercise of legislative discretion to grant an exemption must be founded on some principle of public policy that can support a presumption that the public interest will be served thereby."[46]

The creative developer can take advantage of tax exemption programs that have the goal of providing relief to other institutions. A good illustration of this is provided in *Wein v. Beame,* [47] where a developer took advantage of the tax exemption for property in New York City owned by the Urban Development Corporation (UDC). The developer purchased the dilapidated Commodore Hotel from the Penn Central for $10 million. Thereafter, the developer sold the property to UDC for $1.00. UDC-owned property was eligible for tax exemption. At the same time, the city waived its statutory right to receive from the state an amount equivalent to the taxes that the city would not collect from the Commodore property. UDC then leased the hotel back to the developer for a 99-year term, with the provision that the developer would pay rent not to UDC but to the City. For the first 40 years of the term, the rent would be less than the taxes otherwise due. For the balance of the term, the rent that the developer must pay to the City is equivalent to the taxes he would otherwise have to pay on the property. At the end of the term, title reverts to New York City.

By creative structuring, this developer was able to secure a partial or complete tax abatement for 40 years. Prospective developers are wise to examine all the tax abatement programs available in the relevant jurisdiction to determine if any can be used to the benefit of the proposed project—even those not directly targeted at developers or individual property owners.

Not all commentators agree that tax abatement programs offer real economic incentive to development. One author said:[48]

> Undoubtedly, in areas where property taxes are extremely high, abatement schemes may succeed in inducing some *new* construction that otherwise would not take place. It seems that tax reduction has played a significant role in encouraging commercial construction in downtown Boston, and in making it possible for non-profit and limited-profit sponsors to build moderate housing in Newark. I know of no evidence, however, that property tax abatements anywhere have elicited a significant amount of private market investment in low-income neighborhoods, whether this investment consists of new construction or upgrading existing housing stock.

Although many states have tax abatement programs, they are not universal. The Wisconsin judiciary, for example, has on several occasions invalidated that state's attempt to structure a tax abatement program. In *Gottlieb v. Milwaukee*,[49] the Wisconsin Supreme Court held that a partial exemption from taxes was prohibited by the uniform and equal provisions of the Wisconsin constitution. Under the invalidated Wisconsin statute, property owners were relieved of any tax based on the increment in value attributable to the real estate and any tax that resulted from an increase in value due to certain improvements or buildings on the property.

In another case,[50] the Wisconsin Supreme Court held that a law providing for tax credits for certain improvements allowed certain taxpayers to pay less tax than other similarly situated taxpayers. Thus the court struck down the tax abatement program as violating the Wisconsin prohibition on non-uniform taxes. Indeed, the court implied that partial tax exemptions *in themselves* constitute a violation of Wisconsin law.

Summary

Tax abatement programs offer direct relief to property owners who might otherwise be confronted with significant tax obligations. Unlike TIF programs, which are most beneficial to certain groups of developers, tax abatement programs can be used by all qualifying developers and taxpayers. The higher the taxes the greater the benefit.

Once the obligation to pay property taxes is removed, the developer may be able to afford improvements that would not otherwise be feasible. In addition, the developer may be able to obtain more advantageous financing due to the removal of tax payments from cash flow obligations.

It is sometimes possible for tax abatement programs to be offered for a proposed project as an entity, or for individual components of a project, or through programs targeted to other groups (such as non-profit development corporations).

Developers are advised to consult with local authorities early in the planning process.

HUD Title 10 Programs

Title 10[51] is a federal mortgage insurance program administered by the U.S. Department of Housing and Urban Development (HUD), which is designed to encourage private development of building sites for residential and related uses.[52] The program encompasses acquisition and development of sites for planned unit developments, conventional new subdivisions, and extensions of existing neighborhoods.

The loan proceeds under a Title 10-insured mortgage may be used to finance the purchase of land, and to pay for all customary site improvements, such as water and sewer lines (including water supply and sewage disposal installations), grading, roads, streets,[53] curbs, gutters, sidewalks, and storm drainage.

Title 10 also covers associated land development costs (such as planning fees, surveys, taxes and interest, legal fees, etc.), as well as certain offsite costs, including water and sewer lines, storm drainage, and access roads that are necessary or desirable to develop the site.

Proceeds of the insured mortgage generally may not be used to finance the construction of any building on the site, unless it is a building needed in conjunction with a water supply or sewage disposal installation, or a building (other than a school) that is to be owned and maintained jointly by the property owners.

Development of sites for nonresidential but related uses (industrial, commercial, retail, municipal, religious, educational, etc.) may be included in Title 10 development as long as they are in proper proportion to the scale of the residential project. Recreational facilities such as swimming pools, golf courses, clubhouses, marinas, and tennis courts may be constructed with the proceeds of a Title 10 loan if the residential project is large enough to support such facilities. However, since the thrust of the program is to develop sites for residential communities, funds may not be used to finance development of purely recreational or resort communities, vacation home communities or exclusive subdivisions of luxury housing.

Selection Criteria for Title 10 Housing

The project must represent a "good mortgage risk"[54] and be developed in accordance with an overall development plan. The planned residential project must meet seven general criteria.[55] It must:

- Contribute to sound economic growth
- Provide good living conditions in the area being developed

- Have a sound economic base and a long economic life
- Encourage the maintenance of a diversified local homebuilding industry with broad participation by builders, particularly small builders
- Include a proper balance of housing for low- and moderate-income families
- Be characterized by sound land use patterns
- Include or be served by adequate shopping, school, recreational, transportation, employment and other necessary facilities

Projects should be large enough to constitute a self-contained neighborhood or an orderly extension of an existing neighborhood. There is no minimum project size. The major limitation on project size is a requirement that the number of lots or units in any single-phased project cannot be more than the market area is reasonably capable of absorbing within two years after final endorsement. Development of large acreages may be accomplished in phases, with each new phase requiring a new Title 10 application.

Eligible Mortgagors and Mortgagees[56]

Any entity (individual, partnership, corporation), other than a public body, may apply to HUD for approval as a mortgagor for Title 10 developments. The mortgagor must not engage in any activity other than developing land in the Title 10 project. However, "sponsors" (owners of the mortgagor—whether individuals, partnerships or corporations) may engage in non-Title 10 activities, including constructing housing and facilities in the Title 10 project, as long as they do so through separate corporate entities. Sponsors should not develop projects in competition with their Title 10 projects. Title 10 loans must be obtained from an approved HUD lender.

Mortgage Requirements, Terms and Fees Under Title 10

To be eligible for Title 10 insurance, the mortgage must be on real estate located in the United States[57] and held in fee simple. The only exceptions are for property held under a lease that is for not less than 99 years and is renewable, or under a lease whose term is determined by the Commissioner of Housing to be sufficient to cover the period of development, plus the time period necessary to meet the leasehold eligibility requirements for obtaining FHA financing for the dwelling units to be constructed upon completion of the project. The property must be free and clear of all encumbrances and liens before a Title 10 mortgage will be endorsed for insurance.[58]

The interest accrues at a rate agreed upon by the mortgagor and mortgagee. Interest payments must be made on a monthly basis over the term of the loan. The mortgage term cannot exceed 10 years from the date of the initial endorsement; however, the HUD Secretary may grant an extension of the maturity date where unusual or unforeseen circumstances would cause undue hardship to the mortgagor.[59] No prepayment penalty is permitted.

The mortgagee may not charge a fee for executing and delivering releases of improved lots as they are sold. The lender may require a one-time service charge, not to exceed 2 percent of the mortgage amount, to reimburse the costs of handling and closing the transaction. Mortgage discount points may not be used as a fee in calculating the amount of the mortgage. HUD must approve any other costs or fees required to receive the loan.[60]

There is no specific dollar limit on the mortgage principal allowed under Title 10. However, the principal may not exceed the lesser of:

- 90 percent of the Housing Commissioner's estimate of the development cost, plus 80 percent of the Commissioner's estimate of the value of the land before development
- (a) The Housing Commissioner's estimate of the development costs, plus (b) acquisition cost or all outstanding indebtedness, whichever is greater, plus (c) 50 percent of the difference of the amount used in (b) and the Commissioner's estimate of the value of the land before development
- 85 percent of the Commissioner's estimated value of the property after development, or
- The amount applied for by the mortgagee.[61]

Repayments of principal are generally made on a monthly or quarterly basis once amortization begins. As lots are improved and sold they may be released from the mortgage by a cash payment of 110 percent of that lot's prorated share of the remaining mortgage amount. Release payments must be applied solely to a reduction of principal. At this rate, the loan will be fully repaid when 91 percent of the lots have been released.

At initial endorsement the mortgagor will pay a mortgage insurance base premium of 2 percent of the full amount of the insured loan. This payment covers the first three years of insurance on the loan or the entire term of any mortgage with a term of less than three years. After three years a premium of 1 percent on the outstanding balance is due annually.[62] In order to assure performance under the construction contract, HUD may require the mortgagor to obtain performance and payment bonds or to set up an escrow account with the mortgagee.[63]

The Title 10 Application Process[64]

Processing of Title 10 applications is handled by the local FHA office closest to the project site. Developers should obtain necessary government approvals, such as zoning or land use, before applying for Title 10 insurance. The application process consists of four steps: (1) pre-application conference (2) site approval and market analysis; (3) conditional commitment; and (4) firm commitment.

An applicant may skip any or all of the first three steps. Each succeeding step requires more detailed information about the proposed project. The developer must provide location and zoning maps, cost analyses, environmental reports, the developer's lot sales program, a description of existing easements and utilities, soil tests, engineering studies, and so on.

All applicants are encouraged to arrange a pre-application conference with the local FHA officer. At this conference the developer will explain his/her plans for the project. If the project seems to meet the criteria for a Title 10 project, the local office will ask for a written proposal. The developer may then ask for issuance of a Site Approval and Market Analysis (SAMA) letter. HUD will then conduct a site appraisal and market analysis to determine the initial acceptability of the proposal. Issuance of a SAMA letter does not obligate HUD to insure a mortgage for the proposed project or to issue conditional or firm commitments.

If the results of HUD's initial investigations are positive, the developer may then apply for either a conditional or firm commitment to insure. The major difference in these applications is the degree of finality required in the plans. Issuance of a firm commitment indicates approval of the application for insurance and details the terms and conditions under which the mortgage will be insured.

Special Districts

"Special districts" is a general term that can include any of a number of geographically based jurisdictions created to carry out a specific function or functions. Examples are tax districts, public improvement districts, single-purpose districts, and metropolitan service districts.

Public improvement and metropolitan service districts are most frequently used to finance the construction of infrastructure. There is a major distinction between these two types of districts: public improvement districts are established within the boundaries of an existing municipality, or occasionally a county, while a metropolitan service district is established in an unincorporated area. Public improvement districts are subject to the control of the municipality or county in which they operate, so developers have relatively little control over their creation. Metropolitan service districts are quasi-municipal corporations that operate independently of other jurisdictions. Developers have much more control over the establishment of metropolitan service districts.

Because of the special characteristics of metropolitan service districts, developers use them more frequently to finance infrastructure than the other types of special districts. The discussion below focuses on metropolitan service districts for that reason. The discussion is based on the statutes in Colorado, but other states have similar procedures.

Uses of Metropolitan Service Districts

Metropolitan service districts are used by developers to reduce the front-end costs of providing infrastructure. A metropolitan service district can issue bonds, the proceeds of which are used to pay for the specified infrastructure. General obligation bonds are usually issued.

The tax-exempt status of the bonds is a major attraction to investors. The costs associated with bond financing (beyond the actual cost of the infrastructure) are usually added to the purchase price of the residential units. A combination of property taxes and fees are collected to pay the debt service on the bonds and the operating costs of the district.

Powers of Metropolitan Service Districts

Metropolitan service districts can be used to provide any of a number of services or facilities for a community, such as fire protection, hospital, parks and recreation, water and sanitation services and facilities. Water and sanitation are the services that most frequently motivate developers to consider the creation of a metropolitan service district.

In general, the powers of metropolitan service districts include:

- Entering into contracts and agreements affecting the affairs of the special district
- Borrowing money and incurring indebtedness
- Acquiring, disposing of, and encumbering real and personal property
- Refunding any bonded indebtedness
- Managing, controlling, and supervising all the business and affairs of the district
- Appointing, hiring, and retaining agents, employees, engineers, and attorneys
- Fixing and increasing or decreasing fees, rates, or other charges for services and facilities provided
- Furnishing services and facilities outside the district boundaries and establishing the fees, rates, or charges for those services
- Adopting, amending, and enforcing regulations not in conflict with those of the state

Generally, the taxation power of a metropolitan district is not limited by a maximum revenue or a "rate cap." However, many states have followed the lead of California's Proposition 13 and imposed a limit on the percentage by which a district may increase its taxes in a single year. Metropolitan district rates do need to be market-sensitive, however, to avoid a situation where high rates will limit the competitive marketability of the housing units in the district.

Establishing a Metropolitan Service District

While procedures may vary from state to state, generally the tasks discussed below must be accomplished to establish a metropolitan service district.

If the purpose of a metropolitan service district is to raise the funds necessary to construct and maintain infrastructure, the cost of the infrastructure and its operation must first be determined. This is accomplished through the development of a service plan.

The service plan is often, although not always, prepared by engineers on a consulting basis. A well prepared service plan forms the basis for a financially sound district. The plan should include a detailed itemization of the construction costs for all the infrastructure components, and should project the annual operating costs for the district. The cash flow over the time period when the costs will be incurred should be projected. Anticipated revenues should also be shown in the cash flow analysis, giving the amount of revenues and when they will be received. Revenues generated usually include taxes levied on the property owners, other fees paid by the property owners, and fees paid by the developer. The receipt of these revenues is usually tied to the sale of homes in the district. Therefore, cash flow projections depend on the projections for absorption of the units. In projecting revenues to be generated by payments by property owners, the developer must be careful not to make assumptions about tax rates or fees that would lessen the appeal of the homes to prospective buyers.

The ability to meet the debt service requirements of the bonds is highly dependent on the development and sale of homes. Unimproved land will not generate the required revenues. In the early years of development, debt service often exceeds revenues. In that case, a portion of the proceeds of the bonds may be put in escrow to cover the carrying costs during the development process. The developer may also be required to make a cash contribution.

Once the service plan has been completed and revenue projections have been made, the landowners must petition the county commissioners to create the district. A public hearing will be scheduled. In determining whether to approve the district, the county commissioners will consider the adequacy of the service plan, the results of the public hearing, and other factors. The quality of the service plan is often of paramount importance in the commissioners' decision.

After the county commissioners have approved the district, it is reviewed by the district court. If it meets with the court's approval, an election is held to select a board of directors to manage the district.

Generally, persons who own property in the district and are registered voters of the state are qualified to vote in the metropolitan service district election.

Bonds

Once the district has been established, the developer's attention turns to selling bonds to raise the needed funds. While the projected costs of the district will play the major role in determining the size of the bond offering, the revenues that can be generated by the district must also be considered. The extent to which revenues exceed debt service (the debt coverage ratio) will be of great importance in marketing the bonds to prospective investors. Letters of credit, guarantees and escrowed funds can all increase the marketability of the bonds.

Other Considerations

There are several key characteristics of metropolitan service districts that the developer must consider in deciding whether to use this approach to financing infrastructure. A metropolitan service district is controlled by the qualified electors of the district through the board of directors. This means that as soon as the developer begins to sell land or homes, he/she is no longer in control of the district. The board's desires may differ from those of the developer on a number of significant issues, including the amount of taxes and fees to be paid by the homeowners, the timing of the construction of various portions of the infrastructure facilities, etc. The developer must be prepared to work closely with the board.

As with most financing arrangements, liability must be considered. If the developer has given any guarantees, he/she will share liability with the district. The purchasers of the bonds will have a claim on all improvements within the district. This includes the homes constructed. Therefore, it is often wise to be somewhat conservative in projecting the revenues to be generated by the district. It is perhaps best to build in a cushion when estimating costs, to better assure the ability to cover debt service.

In summary, special districts—and metropolitan service districts in particular—are an important financing strategy for residential infrastructure. This strategy can substantially reduce the developer's front-end costs. But, as with any financing strategy, the issues of risk, funding availability, and project control must be weighed carefully.

Footnotes

1. P.L. 96-499.
2. 26 USC 103A(g).
3. Tax Reform Act of 1986.
4. 1985 Safe Harbor Volume Limits for Mortgage Bonds, Rev. Proc. 85-39.
5. 26 USC 103(b)(4)(A); 26 CFR Section 1. 103-9(b)(5)
6. *Home Building After Tax Reform: A Builder's Guide*, National Association of Home Builders, Washington, D.C., 1986. See also Footnote 3 above.
7. The Treasury Department has amended this definition, effective for bonds issued Jan. 1, 1986 and thereafter, to tailor lower income limit to family size as follows:

    80% of area median income for a family of four or more

    72% of area median income for a family of three

    64% of area median income for a family of two

    56% of area median income for a single-person household

    See also footnote 2 above.
8. The role of the underwriter and substantial portions of the costs of issuance of any bond issue can be substantially reduced by arranging a private placement bond issue or other tax-exempt obligation in lieu of a public sale of bonds on the security market. Private placement is generally structured by a developer or mortgage banker aggressively pursuing and arranging for a private institution—generally a commercial bank—to purchase all the bonds for a particular multifamily project or, in the case of single-family mortgage revenue bonds, to purchase all bonds underwriting permanent mortgage financing for a particular development or geographic area. Since the bonds or equivalent tax-exempt obligation are not sold on the open securities market, the need for an underwriter as a broker for bond sales to private bond buyers is diminished or removed

entirely. Underwriting fees are correspondingly eliminated.
9. North Carolina Housing Finance Agency, Home Ownership Assistance Program.
10. Note that this is true generally with respect to FHA insured issues. For bond issues using other forms of insurance or refined surety or credit enhancement techniques, bond term and lower interest rates can offset any disadvantages gained from the economy of scale by grouping projects into larger periodic issues.
11. HUD Notice 83-58 (December 18, 1983).
12. *Tax Increment Financing: "Rational Basis" or "Revenue Shell Game?"* 22 Urban Law Annual 283, 285 n.18 (1981); *cf* Comment, *Tax Increment Financing: A New Source of Funds for Community Redevelopment in Illinois — People ex re. City of Canton v. Crouch,* 30 DePaul L. Rev. 459 (1981).
13. Davidson, *Tax Increment Financing as a Tool for Community Redevelopment,* 56 J. Urban Law 405, 406 (1979).
14. *Meierhenry v. City of Huron*, 354 N.W.2d 171 (S. Ct. S. D. 1984).
15. Ill. Rev. Stat. ch. 24, 11-74.4-2.
16. Ill. Rev. Stat. ch. 24, 11-74.4-3.
17. *Id* at ch. 24, 11-74.4-3(b).
18. *Id* at ch. 24, 11-74.4-3(1).
19. Proposed legislation currently before the Illinois legislature will add three additional means for qualification as a blighted area:

    (1) The area is subject to chronic flooding;

    (2) The area consists of an unused disposal site containing material removed from construction, demolition, excavation, or dredge sites; or

    (3) The area is between 50 and 100 acres of which 75 percent is vacant (notwithstanding the fact that the area had been used for commercial agriculture within the last 5 years), the area contains one of the four factors qualifying an area as blighted "vacant land," and the area has been designated (but not yet developed) as a town or village center by ordinance or comprehensive plan adopted prior to January 1, 1982.
20. *Id* at ch. 24, 11-74.4-7.
21. *Id* at ch. 24, 11-74.4-9.
22. *Id* at ch. 24, 11-74.4-8.
23. As this book went to press, the Illinois legislature was considering important amendments to the TIF statute. Specifically, the new legislation would allow municipalities to include state sales tax or state utility taxes in the increment to assist in the financing of a redevelopment project. This program would include the following provisions:

    (1) There must be a finding by the municipality that the project would not be developed without such state revenues and that the state revenues will be allocated exclusively to the TIF project development.

    (2) No TIF project can qualify for both sales and utility tax increments. The utility tax increment program is available only for industrial park redevelopment projects.

    (3) The municipality must first utilize the maximum local sales or utility tax allowable to it under Illinois law and must commit all of such tax collected from the TIF district to the Special Tax Allocation Fund.

    (4) The distribution of the increment will be administered by the State Department of Revenue. The Statute will describe the various reporting requirements. The base year for calculating tax increment growth is the calendar year before the TIF ordinance was adopted. For TIF projects adopted before 1985, the base year revenues will equal 1985 revenues generated, less 4 percent for each year that the base year is prior to 1985, not exceeding a total reduction of 12 percent.

    (5) If the initiation of operations in a redevelopment project area by an entity results in the termination of operations by that entity at another location in Illinois, the sales or utility tax liability from the terminated operation shall be added to the base amount for state sales or utility tax increment purposes.

    (6) Only TIF project areas established before January 1, 1987 will be entitled to receive state sales tax increments. TIF project areas created prior to January 1, 1988 shall be eligible for the state utility tax component.

24. See, e.g., *Sigma Tau Gamma Fraternity House Corporation v. City of Menomonee*, 93 Wisc. 2d 393, 288 N.W.2d 85 (1980) (holding that TIF statute does not authorize the city to acquire property but only provides a method of financing).
25. S. Lafer, *Urban Development; An Introductory Guide for Citizens' Groups and Development Agencies,* 56 (1977).
26. See e.g., *People ex. rel. City of Canton v. Crouch*, 79 Ill. 2d 356, 403 N.E.2d 342 (1980).
27. See, e.g., *Tribe v. Salt Lake City Corporation,* 540 P.2d 499 (S. Ct. Utah 1975).
28. *State of Kansas v. The City of Topeka*, 227 Kan. 115, 605 P. 2d 556 (S. Ct. Kan. 1980).
29. *Miller v. Covington Development Authority,* 539 S.W.2d 1 (S. Ct. Ky. 1976).
30. See *Richards v. City of Muscatine,* 237 N.W.2d 48 (Iowa 1975).
31. *Sweetwater Valley Civic Association v. National City,* 18 Cal. 3d 270, 555 P.2d 1099, 1104, 133 Cal. Rptr. 196 (1977).
32. *Id* 555 P.2d at 1104, 133 Cal. Rptr..
33. *Apostle v. City of Seattle,* 70 Wash. 2d 59, 422 P.2d 289 (1966).
34. See also *Regus v. City of Ballwin,* 70 Cal. App. 3d 968, 139 Cal. Rptr. 196 (1977).
35. *Comment, Urban Law Annual, op. cit.* at 289 n.24, citing Schunaff, *An Economic Evaluation of the Used Tax Increment Financing of Urban Renewal in Oregon* (Sept. 1974) (unpublished Ph.D. dissertation in University of Oregon Library).
36. See, e.g., *Southern Valley Grain Dealers Association v. Board of Unity Commissioners of Richland County,* 257 N.W.2d 425 (S. Ct. N.D. 1977).
37. See, e.g., *The Henry Perkins Company v. Board of Assessors of Bridgewater,* 384 N.E. 2d 1241(S. Ct. Mass. 1979).
38. *In re Pyramid Company of Ithaca v. Grievance Board of Tompkins County,* 74 A.D. 2d 970, 425 N.Y.S.2d 883 (1980), appeal dismissed 432 N.Y.S.2d 363.
39. J. Griffith, *Revitalization of Inner City Housing Through Property Tax Exemption and Abatement: New York City's J-51 to the Rescue,* 18 Urban L. Ann 153, 156 (1980).
40. G. Patterson, *The Property Tax and Low Income Housing Markets,* p. 116 in *Property Tax Reform 1973.*
41. NJEDA, *Helping Business Grow & Prosper in New Jersey, A Brief Guide to the Financing Services of the New Jersey Economic Development Authority;* see also, *Vitex Manufacturing Company Ltd. v. The Government of the Virgin Islands,* 351 F.2d 313 (7th Cir. 1965) (discussing tax exemption program of the Virgin Islands). See generally R. Gettel, *You Can Get Your Real Estate Taxes Reduced* (presenting an extensive, then-current 50 state survey of state programs exempting property from taxation).
42. See generally Griffith, *op. cit..*
43. *Dorem Corporation v. Government of the Virgin Islands,* 358 F. 2d 693, 694 (7th Cir. 1966).
44. Griffith, *op. cit.,* p. 192.
45. 71 Am. Jur. 2d State and Local Taxation 319.
46. *Id* at 307.
47. *Wein v. Beame,* 372 N.E.2d 300, 401 N.Y.S.2d 458 (1977).
48. Patterson, *op. cit.,* p. 117.
49. *Gottlieb v. Milwaukee,* 33 Wis.2d 408, 147 N.W.2d 633 (1967).
50. *State ex rel. LaFollette v. Torphy,* 85 Wis. 2d 94, 270 N.W. 2d 187.
51. Title 10 of the National Housing Act, 12 U.S.C. Section 1749 *et. seq.* (1976). See also, 24 C.F.R. Section 205 (1985).
52. For a good, although somewhat dated, discussion of Title 10 compared to other forms of financing for land development and acquisition, see, HOPFL, "Financing Land Development Under Title X," 5 Real Est. Rev. 118 (1975).
53. Private streets may be developed with mortgage proceeds only with prior approval of the Secretary of Housing and Urban Development ("the Secretary"). A maintenance bond will be required of the developer in all projects with private streets. Mortgage proceeds may not be used on streets, parking areas or utilities owned by a condominium association or co-op which can be financed as part of the condominium or co-op's development. *U.S. Department of Housing and Urban Development Handbook 4800.1 Rev. -1, Administration for Title*

X Land Development Projects, (hereinafter *Handbook)* October 1983.
54. 24 C.F.R. Section 205.62 (1985).
55. *Handbook* 2-1.
56. 24 C.F.R. Section 205.30, 205.35 (1985). See also 24 C.F.R. Section 203.10203.4 and 203.6-203.9.
57. For purposes of this Title, the United States includes the several States, Puerto Rico, the District of Columbia, Guam, the Trust Territory of the Pacific Islands, American Samoa and the Virgin Islands.
58. 24 C.F.R. Section 205.42, 205.45 (1985).
59. 24 C.F.R. Section 205.47. A longer maturity date would also be allowed in the case of a privately owned system for water or sewage. See also, 24 C.F.R. Section 205.92 (1985).
60. 24 C.F.R. Section 205.25 (1985).
61. 24 C.F.R. Section 205.55 (1985), also *Handbook* 1-6 at 1-3.
62. 24 C.F.R. Section 2-5.253 (1985).
63. 24 C.F.R. Section 205.82 (1985).
64. See generally 24 C.F.R. Section 205.5 through 205.9 (1985). An application fee is required for the last three steps. 24 C.F.R. Section 205.10 through 205.22 (1985). The second step, the SAMA letter, establishes certain determinations which cannot be changed to the detriment of the applicant if the application for a conditional or firm commitment is received before expiration of the SAMA letter, including the "as-is" value of the land, the completion of an environmental assessment and the estimated absorption period.

Chapter Eight

Selecting a Lender and Preparing the Loan Application

Selecting the Lender

You may choose to go directly to a lender, or to use the professional services of a mortgage banker or broker. Both mortgage brokers and mortgage bankers will professionally package your loan application and place the loan through their contractual—or at least cordial—relationships with banks, savings and loans, private and public Real Estate Investment Trusts (REITs), limited partnerships, and insurance companies. As with any decision regarding an important business relationship, you should gather information and check reliable references before deciding whether to do business with a mortgage banker or broker. Some mortgage bankers fund their own loans and can support all your financial needs, but many are only a conduit for sources of funding not otherwise available to you. Some lenders will do business only through brokers, while others refuse to deal with them.

Whether you are making your application to a lender directly or applying through a mortgage banker or broker, your choice of lender is critical. A concerted effort to select the most receptive and qualified lender for your project prior to loan application will always increase your chances for loan approval. It can save time, effort, and money as well.

You should not make cold-call direct inquiries to lenders initially. This could give the impression that you are "shopping the loan" by just going through the directory for every possible lender. Your inquiry will probably not command serious attention unless it reflects a basic understanding of the lender's funding preferences.

National, regional, and local real estate publications, your local newspaper's business page, and local business periodicals are good sources of information regarding which lenders are active in various sectors of the market.

Start a file and note who's doing what. National subscription services that poll the large lenders are available to provide current information on lender policies. The *Crittenden Report* is one of the simplest comprehensive monthly lists of rates and terms for active lenders.

Another information-gathering technique is to write to the real estate lending departments of any active lenders in your area and ask them to add your name to their mailing list. Talk with other real estate professionals and observe job site signs to determine who is financing what.

Once you understand the basic lending preferences of lenders in your area, you are ready to approach lenders who might be interested in your project and ask them specific questions relating to your proposed project.

Lender preferences are sometimes the result of regulatory influences. All lenders are legally limited in the amount of lending they can do. In most cases, institutions establish their lending preferences based on their expectations of income from particular types of loans. Predetermined geographic factors may limit their interest in certain types of property to a specific area. Often lenders within a particular geographic area vary considerably in their loan preferences.

It is advisable to apply only to institutions that have a preference for the type of loan you are seeking. Regardless of the strength and clarity of your application, it is not likely that you will succeed in persuading a lender to change loan preference policies. The effort is likely to cost you time, and may serve only to demonstrate your lack of understanding of the lending industry.

You may be surprised to learn that some types of lenders periodically run out of funds for investment in real estate loans. Commercial banks, savings and loan associations, and mutual savings banks are especially susceptible to "disintermediation"—commonly called deposit outflows. During periods of general economic downturn, when many depositors are forced to withdraw savings, or when other short-term investment opportunities such as U.S. Treasury bills offer significantly higher interest rates than savings deposits, the lending institutions that rely heavily on savings deposits tend to run short of lending funds. The problem is often compounded when these two factors occur at the same time. When selecting your lender, be sure to consider the current economic condition and the stability of the potential lender's long-term source of funds.

Types of Lending Institutions

The four types of lending institutions most often involved in residential real estate lending are described below. They are commercial banks, savings and loan associations, mutual savings banks, and real estate investment trusts.

Commercial Banks

The 14,000 commercial banks in the United States represent a significant source of funds for land acquisition and development. They vary greatly in their lending capability and activity due to differences in size, in federal and state banking requirements, varied regional banking customs, and individual management preferences.

Many commercial banks are single-location operations, but some have 100 or more branches. Assets of individual commercial banks vary from under $1 million to more than $100 billion. Some larger commercial banks are "wholesale banks," which deal primarily with businesses, while others are "retail banks," which market their services primarily to individuals.

Commercial bank funds available for loans come from four major sources:

- Demand deposits—checking accounts subject to immediate withdrawal.
- Savings and time deposits—funds less subject to immediate withdrawal.
- Capital markets—Banks "purchase" funds in the capital markets by issuing instruments such as commercial paper, notes and bonds.
- Trust funds—The trust departments of banks sometimes invest in real estate mortgage funds that they manage.

Commercial banks make very few long-term real estate loans because such a large portion of their loanable funds are subject to immediate withdrawal. Instead, commercial banks are heavily involved in short-term loans—primarily land and construction loans—where their cash is tied up for shorter periods of time.

Although commercial banks usually are able to lend on any type of real estate, their specific lending policies are adjusted periodically by government regulatory agencies. Generally accepted lending principles have prevailed for some time in the industry, however. If the loan-to-value ratio is very conservative, and the loan maturity period is short, little or no amortization is required. As the loan-to-value ratio and the loan maturity period increase, more amortization is required.

The more the land is improved, the higher the permissible loan-to-value ratio. Unimproved real estate has the lowest loan-to-value ratio; real estate with improved streets and utilities has a slightly higher loan-to-value ratio; and real estate improved with buildings has the highest loan-to-value ratio. Commercial banks are limited in the maximum amount of credit they can extend to one borrower, the maximum size of any one loan, and the percentage of their capital they can invest in all-real estate loans. Commercial banks are allowed to invest only a very small percentage of their assets outside of their geographic market area. In the case of large banks, however, this "small percentage" can represent a large dollar figure.

State-chartered commercial banks operate under a totally different set of laws and regulations than federally chartered banks. Each state determines the laws and regulations under which its state-chartered banks operate.

In an area where branch banking or bank holding companies are available, you should always approach the main banking office or lead bank with a real estate loan request. Branches or small subsidiary banks lack the lending capacity—and usually the expertise—needed to handle real estate lending.

Although commercial banks would rather not let it be known, real estate lending is usually a rather low priority for them because of the cyclical nature of the real estate market and its high degree of risk. The dollar amounts involved in real estate lending are often larger than commercial banks prefer. The financial statements of real estate borrowers are completely different from those of typical commercial bank borrowers.

Savings and Loan Associations

Savings and loan associations are a traditional source of funds for land acquisition and development; in fact these institutions were created to channel savings funds into residential real estate loans.

Savings and loan institutions invest most of their funds in single-family home loans. They are not strongly capitalized; their funds are derived mostly from savings deposits, loan principal repayments, and borrowings from the Federal Home Loan Bank. While the Federal Home Loan Bank Board no longer directly regulates the interest rates that savings and loan associations pay depositors, increased competition from money market funds, government securities, and other savings programs has caused savings and loan associations to lose funds. When large-scale deposit outflows occur, savings and loan associations are usually among the first lending institutions to run out of funds for real estate investment.

Savings and loan associations are chartered by either the federal or state government. A federally chartered savings and loan association must have the word "federal" appear in its name. When the word "federal" does not appear in the name, the savings and loan is a state-chartered institution.

The Federal Home Loan Bank Board regulates the real estate lending activities of federally chartered savings and loan associations. State-chartered savings and loans are regulated by the state government. The lending activities of most savings and loan institutions are geographically restricted to a limited region surrounding their home office or the borders of the home state. Only a very small percentage of their assets may be invested outside their normal lending area, when participating with another savings and loan association located in the area where the borrower lives.

Savings and loan associations will usually loan up to 75 or 80 percent of a development's value, depending on the length of the loan and the payback schedule. Higher loan-to-value ratios generally require a faster payback and a shorter loan term.

Savings and loan associations are permitted to invest in or engage in the direct development of residential subdivisions and their supporting commercial structures. Federally chartered savings and loan associations can invest up to 3 percent of their assets in subsidiaries (service corporations) involved in real estate development activities. These service corporation activities have offered abundant joint venture opportunities to land developers, who give up a percentage of ownership to the service corporation for the necessary equity and the savings and loan's commitment to provide all necessary financing.

The essence of a good joint venture arrangement is a mutuality of desires and complementary abilities. The savings and loan has the money; you, the developer, have ability and control of the land through a contingency or option contract. (See Chapters Four and Six for more information on joint ventures.)

State-chartered savings and loans vary in their involvement in service corporation and joint venture activities. Some states permit their state-chartered savings and loan associations to engage in all the lending activities undertaken by federally chartered institutions. Some states permit even more investment in real estate than federal regulations would allow; others are more restrictive. Check the laws in your state.

Mutual Savings Banks

The approximately 500 mutual savings banks in the United States are a limited but valuable source of funds for land acquisition and development. Mutual savings banks are formidable financial forces in the few states in which they operate; some have deposits of several billion dollars. Mutual savings banks operate primarily in the Northeastern states and in Alaska, Indiana, Minnesota, Oregon, Pennsylvania, Wisconsin and Washington.

Mutual savings banks are not stockholder-owned institutions; they function much like savings and loan associations. While mutual savings banks as such are not federally chartered, some of them have obtained savings and loan association charters from the Federal Home Loan Bank. Mutual savings banks are subject to a wide variety of state regulations. These, along with differences in size, contribute to the diversity of their lending requirements and preferences. Like savings and loans, mutual savings banks exist primarily to provide financing for residential real estate. They are usually restricted to lending in their home state or trade area; only a small percentage of their assets may be loaned outside the primary market area. Mutual savings banks can usually lend up to 75 or 80 percent of the development's fair market value or purchase price (whichever is lower).

Real Estate Investment Trusts

Shaky in the past, but an increasingly reliable source of land acquisition and development funds, real estate investment trusts (REITs) are publicly owned but unincorporated business entities. They are administered by a board of trustees—which functions basically like a corporate board of directors—and are usually associated with a commercial bank, a life insurance company, or a mortgage company.

Equity trust REITs own income-producing properties and benefit from their cash flow and value appreciation. Debt or mortgage trust REITs are lenders that earn their income from fees and interest on real estate loans. Mortgage trust REITs make the land acquisition and development loans needed by residential developers.

Modern REITs emerged in the early 1960s, and were quickly crippled with problems. High interest rates on REIT borrowings put a squeeze on their profits. From the beginning, REITs made long-term, fixed-rate loans funded with short-term borrowings, so when their interest charges increased, trouble ensued. Some REITs were functioning on inadequate underwriting criteria, and issued loan commitments on economically unsound developments. The resulting business failures led to upheaval in the REIT industry, and gave REITs a bad name. The strong, well managed REITs weathered the storm and are still viable lenders.

REITs obtain their investment funds from three major sources:

- Capital markets—funds from the purchase of their shares of beneficial interests
- Short-term borrowing—primarily from commercial banks
- Commercial paper—generally backed by credit lines from commercial banks

All REIT funds available for investment, other than their capital base, are short-term in nature and volatile in cost. It is logical, therefore, for their lending activities to be directed almost exclusively toward shorter-term loans.

REITs are versatile in the types of loans they offer. They are generally interested in any type of income-producing real estate, all types of short intermediate loans and development loans, and even a few long-term loans. They frequently sell participations in their loans to other lenders, such as commercial banks. REITs also structure some joint ventures with borrowers.

REITs are essentially unregulated. They must abide by the case law that has evolved in the states in which they lend, but they are not subject to regulations regarding loan size, structure, type, or geographic area. It is very important to investigate the financial status of any REIT that you are considering as a lender. Talk with their current borrowers, and lenders who have worked with them, to determine whether the REIT is on firm financial footing.

In the process of choosing your lender, it is important to realize that real estate loans are usually the result of a process of negotiation. When there are just a few points to negotiate, the process is relatively short—a benefit to both parties. If a complete restructuring of the deal is required, the negotiation stage can last too long or involve too many issues, so that the lender finds it easier to reject the deal. That is why it is best to deal with lenders who are looking for projects like yours.

Packaging the Loan Submission

You must know ahead of time what information your lender will request, and how to package the information so that it is thorough and easy to understand. A first step is to determine the non-negotiable requirements in the lender's loan approval process. The financing request package is structured around these points. The lender either will not (due to internal policies) or cannot (due to regulatory requirements) yield on these points. For example, no amount of persuasion can make a lender exceed a legally established loan-to-value ratio.

All lenders develop strong individual patterns and formats for their lending policy beyond the legal requirements, from which they will not vary. These individual requirements are often developed as a result of unfavorable lending experiences, so any attempt by you to persuade the lender to deviate from the established format will be viewed with suspicion.

For example, your lender may require a full personal guarantee on all loans, with no room for negotiation. Any request for a variance is considered an effort on your part to get out of your financial responsibility, which creates suspicion. Again, knowing requirements before approaching the lender allows you to tailor your loan submission package to the lender's preferences.

A poorly prepared loan submission package can eliminate any chance of obtaining financing for an otherwise viable development. This is true even if you use a mortgage banker or broker, because first you must gain that banker's or broker's confidence. If you provide inadequate or inaccurate information, the banker or broker will be unable to rewrite the loan submission in the format the investor demands.

Sometimes less is better. A lender would much rather review a concisely written loan request package than wade through mountains of data to find the pertinent facts. The lender uses your loan submission package as the basis for a major financial decision. Give the lender a strong basis for making a decision in your favor. Walk the lender through your development on paper, and back up your statements with facts.

The lender will perform his/her underwriting—that is, confirm your creditworthiness—based on his/her confidence in the financial feasibility of your project and in your ability to perform in a competent manner. Your appearance and personality should at all times reinforce your image as a competent businessperson.

There is no magic format for a loan package, because each must be custom-designed for the borrower, the project, and the lender. A brief description of the elements of a typical loan submission package follows.

Cover Letter

The cover letter should summarize the loan request and the contents of the loan submission package. Keep the letter short and very positive in tone.

Loan Summary

The loan summary describes the transaction to enable the lender to decide quickly if it meets the institution's basic requirements. Outline the collateral, the borrower, and the required financing. Length of one page is recommended.

The Borrower

Even if the loan officer has known you your whole life, sell hard in this section with facts attesting to your capabilities. You need to demonstrate conclusively that you (the borrower) can complete this proposed project.

If you have no previous experience with the lender, they will probably require documentary evidence of your technical and financial ability to complete the proposed project. Information on your banking relationships, creditworthiness, and references from those who have done business with you (such as architects, contractors, building materials suppliers) are often required.

Market Data

This section should be tailored to the scope and location of the project. For smaller projects, a few pages of data you have collected yourself may suffice. For large and complex developments, a professional narrative appraisal or feasibility report might be used. A very positive conclusion regarding the project's desirability and feasibility is needed.

Project Data

The site and the proposed improvements should be presented in as much detail as necessary to show that the proposed project is equal to or superior to existing products in the market.

The lender will typically need the following information about the project, which should be briefly summarized in the body of the application, with actual documentation provided in an Appendix:

- A map of the project
- Detailed plans and specifications for the units
- A site plan
- A project cost statement
- Soil conditions report
- Zoning approval documentation
- Assurance of utility availability

Financial Proformas

Walk your lender through the numbers. Do a cash flow analysis: show how much money is needed and when it will be spent; show how much money will be earned and when it will come in. Be realistic and conservative because these numbers play a big role in the negotiations regarding the cost of the loan. If you have done your homework, you will have already plugged into your numbers the points and rates the lender is looking for, or at least close approximations.

Expect the lender to attempt to verify your construction cost estimates by comparing them to industry standards.

Construction lenders generally require loan guarantees. Lenders often require developers to give personal guarantees (pledge personal assets) to assure the successful completion of the project, particularly where the developer has established a "one-shot" or "shell" corporation for the development of a single project. First-time developers are usually required to obtain a performance bond and a labor and materials bond, which assure the lender that funds will be available to finish the project should the developer fail to perform.

Lenders frequently require a property appraisal at the time of project completion. The appraisal verifies that the project has been completed according to plan. The reliability of appraisal reports has become a major issue in construction financing because the reports are used to measure the project's success and effectively determine the viability of the loan commitment.

Appendix

This should include all the data supporting what you have presented, including the bulky plans and documents.

Again, there is no set formula for loan submission packages. This is a creative area in the financial field. Take it as a challenge to create a communications tool that will convince your loan officer that he or she should approve your loan.

An application form for a land acquisition and development loan, or a joint venture, is shown in the Appendix to this book. It is a detailed form that, if properly filled out and accompanied by the necessary documents, can give the lender all the information needed to underwrite a loan. The form is a sample only, but it is a useful guide to collection and organization of the information necessary for a formal submission to a lender.

Loan Commitment and Closing

The lender decides whether to fund your project based on an analysis of the project and financial information you submit. If the decision is favorable, the lender will send you a commitment letter spelling out the terms of the loan. If the terms are acceptable to you, and if you are able to fulfill any additional requirements the lender may note, loan closing can occur.

At closing both lender and developer sign loan agreements documenting the obligations each party has agreed to assume. Some of the elements commonly included in loan agreements are:

- A loan entitlement clause that requires the developer to pay interest on the amount of the loan proceeds to which he/she would have been entitled on the basis of the construction schedule, whether or not the loan advance is actually made
- A statement that requests for loan advances will constitute an affirmation that all of the representations made at the time of the agreement are still true
- A requirement that loan advances will be made according to actual construction progress and the construction line budget, rather than by a calendar schedule
- A clause requiring assurances that utility services are in place or will be available.

Summary

From the time you begin negotiations with the seller of the land, you are dealing with factors that will have an impact on the method you use to finance your land acquisition and development. You must select the method of financing that is best for your project, and a lender whose policies, procedures, and demands match the needs of the project.

Your success or failure in securing financing will depend on how well you research your lender's priorities, and how well you communicate the merits of your project and its financial requirements to the lender. A well thought-out financing strategy presented to an appropriate lender in a high-quality, comprehensive, but concise loan request package has the best chance of success.

Appendix

Appendix 5-A
Standard Land Purchase Contract

1. THIS AGREEMENT is made this _____ day of _____,
   , between   , an
Corporation, hereinafter "Seller" and
              , an   Corporation, hereinafter
"Buyer" for the purchase and sale of the following
described property:

at the price of

2. THE EARNEST MONEY. Buyer shall pledge those
payments due him as of the date of this Agreement under
a separate agreement with Seller entitled Development
and Marketing Agreement dated   , for the
development of the property known as
(hereinafter "   ") as earnest money to be
applied on the purchase price.

3. THE CLOSING DATE. The earlier of
or five (5) days after Seller acquires title to the
Property from the
              , shall be the closing date and closing
shall be held at

4. POSSESSION. Possession shall be granted to Buyer at closing.

5. THE DEED. Seller shall convey or cause to be conveyed to Buyer or his nominee, by a recordable, stamped general warranty deed or by corporate deed, good title to the premises subject only to the following "permitted exceptions" if any: (a) General real estate taxes for   and subsequent years; (b) Building, building line and use or occupance restrictions, conditions and covenants of record; (c) Zoning laws and Ordinances; (d) Easements for public utilities; (e) Drainage ditches, feeders, laterals and drain tile, pipe or other conduit; (f)

Terms provisions, covenants, and conditions of the subdivision documentation and all amendments thereto; any easements established by or implied from the said documentation, if any. (g) Special assessments or taxes for improvements not yet completed or instalked and unconfirmed taxes or assessments.

6. FINANCING. Seller shall obtain, for the benefit of Buyer, from   , on the   day of closing, a loan in the total amount of   to be secured by the Property and improvements to be completed thereon. Interest from time to time on the unpaid balance shall be at the rate of no more than   over the prime rate as published from time to time by Chase Manhattan Bank of New York or, if Chase Mangattan Bank of New York ceases to publish a prime rate, by City Bank of New York with no service charge or points. There shall be a release fee of   to be paid to   upon the partial release of the mortgage of any lot in the Property on which Buyer has constructed an improvement consisting of a single family home held for resale. No release fee shall be due upon the sale of any lot without such an improvement. The loan proceeds shall be disbursed as follows:

    A. The sum of

less that amount set forth below as required down payment, for the acquisition of the Property on the day of closing;

B. Such sums as may be necessary, up to the full total amount of the loan, for the direct and indirect costs of developing and constructing improvements upon the Property, and all soft costs including, but not limited to, management fees, interest, discounts, and marketing expenses, paid or incurred from time to time in accordance with the documentation requirements of   & Loans' construction loan department.

7. REQUIRED DOWN PAYMENT. Buyer shall make a contribution to the acquisition price of the Property (hereinafter "Required Down Payment") in an amount required by   but in no event greater than

                                                    . The Required Down Payment shall consist of (1) the earnest money previously credited hereunder and (2) an advance from Seller to Buyer of such additional sums as may become due Buyer under the   to equal, together, the Required Down Payment. No funds shall pass between Buyer and Seller, however, the books and records of Buyer and Seller in connection with the shall be adjusted in accordance with the credit to Seller for the Required Down Payment, hereunder.

8. TITLE. Seller shall furnish or cause to be furnished to Buyer at Seller's expense a commitment issued by   to issue an owner's title insurance policy on the current form of American Land Title Association Owner's Policy (or equivalent policy) including coverage over General Schedule B exceptions in the amount of the purchase price covering the date hereof, subject only to: (1) the "permitted exceptions" as set forth in Paragraph 6, (2) title exceptions pertaining to liens of encumbrances of a definite or ascertainable amount, which may be removed by the payment of money at the time of closing (an amount sufficient to secure the release of such title exceptions shall be deducted from the proceeds of Seller).

9. AFFIDAVIT OF TITLE. Seller shall furnish Buyer at closing with an Affidavit of Title, covering the date of closing, subject only to those permitted special exceptions set forth in Paragraph 6, and unpermitted exceptions, if any, as to which the title insurer commits to extend insurance in the manner specified in Paragraph 8.

10. PRORATIONS. General real estate taxes shall be prorated as of the closing date on the basis of the tax assessor's latest equalized assessed valuation times the latest known tax rate. All provisions shall be final.

11. PERFORMANCE. Time is of the essence of this contract.

12. SURVEY, PLANS AND ENGINEERING DOCUMENTS. At closing, Seller shall deliver to Buyer a survey certified by a licensed surveyor, having all corners staked and showing all improvements existing as of this contract date, and all easements and building lines, and such plans, specifications and engineering documents as are then in Seller's possession.

13. RISK OF LOSS. In the event that, prior to closing, all or any of the Property shall be substantially destroyed by fire or other casualty, or in the event any portion of the subject premises shall be taken by governmental action through condemnation, then, at the option of either party hereto, this Contract shall be declared null and void, and the Buyer shall be entitled to a return of all monies paid hereunder, together with interest hereon.

14. BROKERS COMMISSION. It is understood that   is entitled to a brokerage commission of   of the sale price which shall be credited against the required down payment.

15. SELLERS REPRESENTATIONS. Seller represents and warrants that the Property currently consists of

               and that Seller has no knowledge of any factor which would prevent the Property from being developed in accordance with the requirements of those zoning classifications.

16. REPRESENTATIONS REGARDING CONSIDERATION. Buyer has entered into this contract in consideration for the provision of a loan from   as set forth hereinbefore.

16. ENTIRE AGREEMENT. This constitutes the entire agreement between the parties.

17. This contract shall be construed in accordance with the laws of the State of Illinois.

Buyer: Seller:

By:_____   By:_____

ILL85523Y 11/23/85

Appendix 5-B
Option Contract

OPTION given this _____ day of _____, 1985, by   not individually but as trustee under its trust number 7-1218 dated _____, 19__, OPTIONOR, to
         , not individually but as promoter for an Illinois Corporation yet to be formed and to be named   , OPTIONEE.

    1. GRANT OF OPTION. Optionor, in consideration of one hundred dollars ($100.00) in hand paid, receipt of which is acknowledged by optionor, grants to optionee the exclusive right and option to purchase, on the following terms and conditions the real property in DuPage County, Illinois, described as follows:

    2. OPTION PERIOD. The term of this option shall commence on the date of this agreement and shall continue until _____, 1988, except that the option shall terminate on _____, 1986, in the event OPTIONEE has not exercised the option on no fewer

than three lots on the Property before that date.

3. PURCHASE PRICE OF PROPERTY. The full purchase price of the Property is   which amount shall be payable in separate and distinct segments of Twenty Thousand Dollars ($20,000.00) per lot as hereinafter provided if and to the extent that an OPTIONEE elects to exercise this option.

4. APPLICATION OF CONSIDERATION TO PURCHASE PRICE. If OPTIONEE purchases the Property or any lot of the Property described in this option, and under the terms and conditions hereof, the consideration hereunder shall be applied, proportionately, to each lot purchase allocating one-eight of the consideration to each lot.

5. EXERCISE OF OPTION. OPTIONEE may exercise this option by giving OPTIONOR written notice thereof, signed by OPTIONEE, as to all or any part of the Property, so long as no notice requires the conveyance of less than one (1) full lot as set forth in the subdivision plat. Upon such notice, OPTIONOR shall permit OPTIONEE access to the Property or any part of the Property designated in such notice and OPTIONEE shall be permitted to construct an improvement thereon.

6. SALE OF IMPROVEMENT AND PAYMENT OF PURCHASE PRICE. OPTIONEE shall exercise its best efforts to market and sell the improvements so constructed on lots on the Property by it. OPTIONOR shall, if necessary, pledge the Property or any part of the Property to secure any construction loan obtained by OPTIONEE for the improvement of the property. OPTIONEE may enter into contracts in its own name to sell the lots and the improvements. OPTIONOR shall join in the execution of any and all documents necessary to effect the construction of improvements on the lots and the sale of those lots and improvements to third parties, including, if necessary, the execution of loan documents, provided that OPTIONOR shall not be personally liable on any construction loan obtained by

OPTIONEE. Upon the closing of the sale of a lot and improvement to a third party, OPTIONOR shall, if so directed by OPTIONEE, convey title to that third party rather than to OPTIONEE. OPTIONEE shall pay OPTIONOR at the time of the closing of the sale of a lot to a third party and as full consideration for that lot the sum of Twenty Thousand Dollars ($20,000.00), plus or minus prorations, which shall be paid to OPTIONOR out of the proceeds of the sale.

    7. NOVATION. Upon issuance of a Certificate of Incorporation for   , OPTIONOR and OPTIONEE shall enter into a contract of novation with   , rendering that corporation the liable party hereunder and releasing   from any personal liability hereunder.

    8. PROOF OF TITLE. OPTIONOR shall, at his expense, furnish OPTIONEE a policy of title insurance, written by Title Services, Inc. insuring the title to the property to be free and clear of all defects except those specifically mentioned herein together with each conveyance hereunder. Title to the property shall be conveyed free and clear of all encumbrances except those disclosed on a tract search provided by OPTIONOR and acceptable to OPTIONEE within five (5) days of the date hereof.

    The real property taxes on the Property, whether a lien or not, assessed or to be assessed for the year in which this transaction is finally consummated shall be prorated between the parties to the date of delivery of the deed of conveyance, the amount of the prior year's taxes shall then be used as a basis of proration. All special assessments and special ad valorem levies, if any, shall be paid by OPTIONOR whether the same be payable in a lump sum, in installments, or otherwise.

    9. NOTICES. All notices provided for herein shall be deemed to have been duly given if and when deposited in the United States mail, properly stamped and addressed to the party for whom intended at the party's above listed address, or when delivered

personally to such party.

　　　10.　TIME OF ESSENCE.　Time is of the essence of this option.

　　　11.　BINDING EFFECT.　This option shall be binding upon and shall inure to the benefit of the parties hereto and to their respective heirs, successors, or assigns.

CELLUCCI & YACOBELLIS, ATTORNEYS
1155 SOUTH WASHINGTON
NAPERVILLE, IL 60540
(312) 961-0225

Appendix 5-C
Land Installment Contract

1. THIS AGREEMENT is made this _____ day of _____, _____, between _____, referred to as "Buyer" and _____, as Trustee under Trust Number _____, hereinafter referred to as "Seller," for the purchase and sale of the following described property:

Parcel A:

and

Parcel B:

at the price of

2. SIGNS. At the time of closing, Seller shall transfer all permits and agreements for on or off-site installation.

3. THE EARNEST MONEY. Buyer shall pay _____ as earnest money to be applied on the purchase price. The earnest money shall be held in an interest-bearing account, with interest payable to Buyer, payable at the joint direction of counsel for Buyer and Seller for the mutual benefit of the parties concerned and upon the closing of the sale, shall be applied to the purchase price.

4. THE CLOSING DATE.

5. POSSESSION. Possession shall be granted to Buyer at closing.

6. THE DEED. Seller shall convey or cause to be conveyed to Buyer or his nominee, by a recordable, stamped general warranty deed, good title to the premises subject only the following "permitted exceptions" if any: (a) General real estate taxes for   and subsequent years; (b) Building, building line and use or occupance restrictions, conditions and covenants of record; (c) Zoning laws and Ordinances; (d) Easements for public utilities; (e) Drainage ditches, feeders, laterals and drain tile, pipe or other conduit; (f) Party walls, party wall rights and agreement; covenants, conditions and restrictions of record; terms provisions, covenants, and conditions of the Declaration of Conditions, Covenants, Restrictions, Grants, and Easements recorded as Document Number   , and all amendments thereto; any easements established by or implied from the said Declaration of Condominium or amendments thereto.

7. FINANCING. Seller shall extend to Buyer, on the day of closing, a loan in the amount of

memorialized on the form attached hereto as Exhibit A, and secured by a purchase money mortgage on Parcel A.

8. TAKEOUTS AND PARTIAL RELEASES. Buyer shall pay to Seller the sum of
                                upon the sale of any improved site in Parcel A. Upon such payment, Seller shall issue a partial release of mortgage on such lot.

9. PAYMENT OF INTEREST. Buyer shall pay Seller interest at the rate of   percent   per annum on the monies outstanding from time to time on the note referenced in Paragraph 7 hereof on the last day of each calendar year beginning with   , and continuing annually until all funds are fully repaid. Nothing contained herein shall affect Seller's obligation to issue releases under the terms of Paragraph 8 hereof.

10. DEVELOPER. Seller represents that it has the position of developer in accordance with the beforementioned Declaration of Conditions and that such position is transferrable as to those portions of the development being transferred hereunder without any amendment to the obligations of developer thereunder and shall effect such a transfer of position in an orderly fashion with appropriate documentation acceptable to Buyer's counsel.

11. BUILDING PERMITS. Before closing, Seller shall obtain written assurances from the   that building permits are issuable in connection with the subject lots and Seller shall pay all currently outstanding engineering fees and obtain all engineering reports necessary to assure that the   will issue such building permits.

12. HOMEOWNERS ASSOCIATION. Seller represents and warrants that the Homeowners Association defined in the before-mentioned Declaration of Conditions has not been formed by recording Articles of Incorporation with the Illinois Secretary of State.

13. IMPROVEMENTS. Seller represents and warrants that the partial improvements on Parcel B and the foundations on Parcel A are buildable using customary construction procedures as contemplated by the plans, specifications, and blueprints to be provided by Seller under the terms of Paragraph 19 hereof and without the requirement of removal.

14. TITLE. Seller shall furnish or cause to be furnished to Buyer at Seller's expense a commitment issued by a title insurance company licensed to do business in   , to issue an owner's title insurance policy on the current form of American Land Title Association Owner's Policy (or equivalent policy) including coverage over General Schedule B exceptions in the amount of the purchase price covering the date hereof, subject only to: (1) the "permitted exceptions" as set forth in Paragraph 6, (2) title exceptions pertaining to liens or encumbrances of a definite or ascertainable amount, which may be removed by the payment of money at the time of closing (an amount sufficient to secure the release of such title exceptions shall deducted from the proceeds of Buyer).

15. INDEMNIFICATIONS. Seller shall hold harmless and indemnify Buyer from and against any and all actions taken by Seller or Seller's beneficiaries or predecessors in connection with the subject property before the date of transfer of title to Buyer hereunder. Buyer shall hold harmless and indemnify Seller from and against any and all actions taken by Buyer or Buyer's beneficiaries or predecessors in connection with the subject property after the date of transfer of title hereunder.

16. AFFIDAVIT OF TITLE. Seller shall furnish Buyer at closing with an Affidavit of title, covering the date of closing, subject only to those permitted special exceptions set forth in Paragraph 6, and unpermitted exceptions, if any, as to which the title insurer commits to extend insurance in the manner specified in Paragraph 14.

17. PRORATIONS. General real estate taxes shall be prorated as of the closing date on the basis of the tax assessor's latest equalized assessed valuation times the latest known tax rate, subject to a reproration upon receipt of the tax bill.

18. PERFORMANCE. Time is of the essence of this contract.

19. SURVEY, PLANS, SPECIFICATIONS, AND BLUEPRINTS. Prior to closing date, Seller shall deliver to Buyer or his agent a survey of the premises, along with all plats of subdivision, certified by a licensed surveyor, having all corners staked and showing all improvements existing as of this contract date, and all easements and building lines, the blueprints for the partial improvement on Parcel B, and the plans and specifications for the improvements originally intended to be constructed on the two foundations currently on Parcel A.

20. RISK OF LOSS. In the event that, prior to closing, all or any of the improvements shall be substantially destroyed by fire or other casualty, or in the event any portion of the subject premises shall be taken by governmental action through condemnation, then, at the option of Buyer this Contract shall be declared null and void, and the Buyer shall be entitled to a return of all monies paid hereunder, together with interest hereon.

21. BROKERS COMMISSION. It is understood that no real estate commission is due.

22. ENTIRE AGREEMENT. This constitutes the entire agreement between the parties.

23. This contract shall be construed in accordance with the laws of the State of

24. TRUST BENEFICIARIES. The undersigned beneficial interest holders and holders of power of direction of Seller trust hereby guarantee the obligations of Seller hereunder and assume all obligations of Seller hereunder as though said holders were Seller.

Buyer: Seller:

By: _____   By: _____

                                                 _____

Appendix 5-D
Phased Land Purchase Contract

(RIDER TO REAL ESTATE SALE CONTRACT BY AND BETWEEN   PURCHASER AND   NOT PERSONALLY BUT AS TRUSTEE UNDER TRUST NO.   , SELLER)

10. Notwithstanding anything to the contrary herein contained, it is understood that the purchase price herein is based upon THIRTY FIVE THOUSAND ($35,000.00) DOLLARS per acre and that upon Seller's obtaining the survey as provided for hereunder, said purchase price shall be adjusted accordingly to reflect the true acreage of the property.

11. It is further understood that Purchaser shall have a period of forty-five (45) days from the date of execution hereof to enter upon the subject property for the purpose of taking soil boring tests. Purchaser agrees to indemnify and hold harmless Seller from any and all liability resulting from or as a result of the aforesaid soil boring tests. In the event that Purchaser determines within said thirty (30) days, and so notifies Seller in writing within said period of time, that said soil boring tests have proved unsatisfactory to Purchaser, then in such event, Purchaser shall be entitled to cancel the within Agreement and receive return of all monies on deposit hereunder as well as

interest earned thereon, provided however, that Purchaser shall provide Seller with copies of any such soil tests.

12. Purchaser agrees within forty-five (45) days of execution hereof to provide Seller with a proposed plan of development for the subject property. It is understood that this Agreement is contingent upon the Seller obtaining within one hundred and fifty (150) days of the date of execution of this Agreement annexation of the subject property to the Village of Streamwood and rezoning of same by said Village as well as approval to develop the subject property in said Village pursuant to its planned unit development ordinance in substantial conformance with the plan heretofore provided by Purchaser to Seller. In the event that Seller fails to obtain said approvals for Purchaser within said time period, Purchaser may at its option notify Seller, within said time period of its intention to cancel the within Agreement in which event Purchaser shall be entitled to the return of all monies on deposit and interest earned thereon.

13. Initial closing shall be held fourteen (14) days after Seller notifies Purchaser, in writing, that all contingencies hereunder have been satisfied or waived. Upon such notification, Purchaser shall, within seven (7) days designated a portion of the entire parcel referenced in Paragraph 1 of the contract to which this Rider is attached (hereinafter Entire Parcel) to be conveyed at the Initial

Closing, all in accordance with the terms hereof, which shall be a portion no less than one-third of the acreage of the Entire Parcel for which Purchaser shall pay a proportion of the purchase price equal to the ratio of the acreage of the portion so designated to the acreage of the Entire Parcel.

14. From time to time, after the date of the Initial Closing and before the first anniversary of that date, Purchaser may designate, in writing, by notice to Seller, further portions of the Entire Parcel for conveyance (hereinafter Designated Portions), provided however, that said Designated Portions shall be not less than five (5) acres. Within fourteen (14) days of such notice, Seller shall convey, all in accordance with the terms hereof, such Designated Portions for which Purchaser shall pay a proportion of the purchase price equal to the ratio of the acreage of the Designated Portion to the acreage of the Entire Parcel plus an amount equal to ten (10%) percent interest per annum from the date of the Initial Closing to the date of the conveyance of the Designated Portion on that proportion of the purchase price paid in connection with the conveyance of the Designated Parcel.

15. From time to time, after the date of the Initial Closing and before the second anniversary of that date, Purchaser may elect, in writing, by notice to Seller, to purchase the entire balance of the Entire Parcel. Within

fourteen (14) days of such notice, Seller shall convey, all in accordance with the terms hereof, the balance of the Entire Parcel for which Purchaser shall pay the balance of the purchase price plus an amount equal to ten (10%) percent interest per annum from the date of the Initial Closing to the date of the conveyance of the balance of the Entire Parcel on that proportion of the purchase price paid in connection with the conveyance of the balance of the Entire Parcel.

16. Purchaser shall have no obligation to pay the interest referred to in the above paragraphs 14 and 15 until and unless Purchaser takes title to a further Designated Portions after the date of the Initial Closing and, upon such conveyances, only to the extent that the interest accrues against the proportion of the purchase price paid for that Designated Portion. It is further expressly understood and agreed that Purchaser shall have no obligation to designate any portion of the property for further conveyance beyond that property designated for conveyance at the Initial Closing and that, at the expiration of two (2) years after the date of the Initial Closing, both Seller and Purchaser shall be released from any obligation to convey or purchase any portion of the Entire Parcel concerning which Purchaser has not previously notified Seller that that portion is part of a Designated Portion.

17. All Designated Portions shall be contiguous to a previously conveyed or designated portion and all portions designated either for conveyance at the Initial Closing or for subsequent conveyance shall run the entire width of the Entire Parcel from   to the western border of the Entire Parcel. It is further understood that notwithstanding anything to the contrary herein contained, each partial conveyance of the Entire Parcel shall be adjusted to provide that the ratio that the acreage of the property conveyed bears to the acreage of the Entire Parcel shall be proportional to the ratio that the number of units in the proposed plan of development for that portion of the acreage so conveyed bears to the number of units for the entire proposed plan of development.

18. It is further agreed that on or before initial closing, Seller shall cause sewer and water service to be brought to the site at Seller's sole cost and expense, provided however, that Seller shall be entitled to retain any and all rights of recapture in connection with the subject property except that Purchaser shall not be liable for any recapture payment to Seller or to the Municipality. Purchaser shall be responsible for any and all usual and customary annexation fees, municipal contributions and/or dedications required in conjunction with its plan.

19. This Agreement shall be binding upon and inure to the benefit of the parties hereto and their respective successors and assigns.

PURCHASER:

BY: _____

SELLER:

BY: _____

CELLUCCI & YACOBELLIS, ATTORNEYS
1155 SOUTH WASHINGTON
NAPERVILLE, IL 60540
(312) 961-0225

Appendix 7-A
Tax Increment Financing (TIF)

Statutes for Indiana, Minnesota, Ohio, California, and Florida

Indiana

The Indiana TIF statute allows municipalities and counties, except "townships," to use tax-increment financing to redevelop blighted areas within their jurisdiction. The statute anticipates that municipalities and counties will acquire blighted property and will fund redevelopment through the issuance of bonds.[1] Such bonds are retired with funds collected from incremental real estate tax revenues and/or revenues from a "special tax." Significantly, the statute envisions projects with and without the involvement of private developers.

A five-person municipal redevelopment commission is empowered to acquire, hold, sell, lease, or grant interests in all or part of the real property needed for the redevelopment of the blighted area "on the terms and conditions that they consider best for the [governmental] unit and its inhabitants."[2]

The commission is also authorized to clear any property, repair or maintain structures, or remodel, rebuild, enlarge or make structural improvements to any structures acquired for redevelopment purposes.

Finally, the commission may also contract for the construction of public ways, sidewalks, sewers, waterlines, parking facilities, park or recreational areas, or other public improvements necessary for the redevelopment of blighted areas within the corporate boundaries of the relevant governmental unit.

Indiana's TIF procedures are straightforward. As in Illinois, the redevelopment commission must reach certain substantive conclusions before a TIF can be authorized. The commission must reach two conclusions: That an area under their jurisdiction is so blighted that the normal governmental regulatory processes or the independent initiative of private enterprise will not eradicate the blight; and that the public health and welfare will be benefited by the acquisition and redevelopment of any such area.

After such substantive findings have been made, the commission may prepare:

- Maps and plats outlining the boundaries of the blighted area, the location of the various parcels of property, streets and other features affecting the acquisition, clearance, replatting, replanning, rezoning, or redevelopment of the area; and
- Separate appraisals by at least two independent appraisers of the fair value of the parcels of property proposed to be acquired. These appraisals are not open to public inspection.[3]

Based on its findings, the commission must adopt a resolution "declaring that the blighted area is a menace to the social and economic interest of the unit and its inhabitants, and that it will be of public utility and benefit to acquire the area and redevelop it under this statute."

The resolution must also include the estimated cost of acquiring the blighted areas, as determined by averaging the fair market value of the blighted area as established by the two separate, independent appraisers.[4]

The statute gives no explicit definition of the term "blighted areas." In *Hawley v. South Bend Department of Redevelopment*, however, Indiana's Supreme Court focused on the South Bend Redevelopment Commission resolution that, in anticipation of the development of a new shopping center, declared that the South Bend business district was "blighted."[5]

The Court concluded that an independent consultant's finding of blight, a separate Chamber of Commerce survey also indicating blight, and an official Commission finding of blight were sufficient evidence to "support the findings of blight."[6]

As evidence of "severe economic stagnation of the downtown business district [i.e. blight]," these reports cited the following facts: 22 businesses had relocated from the district in recent years; the share of retail dollars spent in the district had been rapidly declining; and no willing purchasers came forward for property previously acquired by the Redevelopment Commission. These facts demonstrated the "lack of development [and a] cessation of growth which have made the area described as blighted under current conditions undesirable for or impossible for normal development and occupancy."[7]

After adopting a resolution declaring an area "blighted," the Redevelopment Commission must submit its plan to the appropriate legislative body (the city council or board of trustees or the county board of supervisors). This body then develops a general plan for development of the blighted area. The resolution and the redevelopment plan are then amended or modified, if necessary, to conform with the relevant governmental unit's comprehensive plan. After approval by the Planning Commission or other appropriate agency, public hearings are held before the Redevelopment Commission. The Commission takes final action after considering the evidence presented at the public hearings and determining whether the proposed redevelopment plan will benefit the public sufficiently. The Commission's action is final unless an appeal is filed within ten days.[8]

The Commission can then acquire property in the redevelopment area. The prices offered to owners of each parcel may not exceed the average of the fair market value established by two independent appraisals. The Commission, however, may assume the expenses of title examination and conveyance of the property. The Commission also has the authority to acquire any real property in a blighted area by applying to the governmental unit it represents to initiate eminent domain proceedings.

Initially, the property is offered for sale or lease through a competitive, public bidding format. The offering prices for the property may not be less than the average of the fair market value determined by the independent appraisals. Appropriate notice of the sale is required. At the time cited in the notice, the Commission may receive offers and make awards to the "highest and best bidders."[9] In determining the "best bids," the Commission must consider some or all of the following factors:

- The size and character of the improvements proposed to be made by the bidder on the real property bid on
- The bidder's ability to improve the property with reasonable promptness
- Whether the property, when improved, will be sold or rented
- The bidder's proposed sale or rental prices
- Any other facts that will further the execution of the redevelopment plan[10]

The Commission may make its award based on compliance with certain conditions relating to these factors. Further, any redevelopment agreement may also require surety bonds, good faith deposits, liquidated damages, the right of repurchase, or other rights and remedies that go into effect if the bidder fails to comply with the Commission's terms.

If some of the property within the blighted area remains unsold, the Commission may dispose of it either at public sale or through private negotiation. For 90 days after the opening of the written offers, however, no sale or lease may be consummated for a price or rental less than that shown on the offering sheet. The exception is for sale or rental of ten or more parcels to a single purchaser or lessee, who agrees to improve the parcels immediately. In that case, the Commission is empowered to adjust the offering price as it deems necessary to further the redevelopment plan.

The redevelopment plan is funded through the collection of property taxes within the redevelopment area. In anticipation of the taxes to be levied and allocated in the redevelopment area, the Commission may, by resolution, issue bonds. The bonds must mature within 50 years of their issuance, and the total amount of bonds must not exceed the Commission's estimate of all the acquisition costs associated with the property. Acquisition costs include, but are not limited to, the acquisition costs for all the property and rights-of-way to be redeveloped and all the necessary architectural, engineering, legal, accounting, advertising, bond discount, and supervisory expenses.

The Commission may use tax allocation financing [tax increment financing] to pay the principal and interest on any bonds issued. If the resolution authorizing the use of tax increment financing is passed, the Commission may declare all—or a part—of the redevelopment area an "allocation area" and require that any property taxes subsequently levied on taxable property in the allocation area shall be allocated and distributed as follows:

- The proceeds of the taxes attributable to the assessed value of all the property, as determined by the most recent assessment taken before the effective date of the allocation provision of the resolution, shall be allocated to the respective taxing units.
- All property tax proceeds in excess of those described above shall be allocated to the redevelopment district and, when collected, paid into a special fund for that allocation area.[11]

If the bonds are payable solely from the tax proceeds allocated as described above, they may be issued in any amount without limitation.

Alternately, or in addition, the Commission may levy a "special" tax on all of the property in the redevelopment district, and use the revenues to retire the bonds. This tax may not exceed 10 cents per $100 of taxable valuation for a municipality, or 4 cents per $100 of taxable valuation for a county.[12] The statute contemplates combined use of the special tax and tax allocation methods only when the tax allocation method will not yield sufficient revenues to pay off the bonds. If both tax approaches are used, the amount of special tax levied is to be reduced by any excess amount available in the allocation funds attributable to the tax allocation approach. Additionally, if the special tax method is implemented, the total value of any bonds issued for initial project funding may not exceed 2 percent of the total assessed valuation of property in the redevelopment district.

Minnesota

The Minnesota statute is very similar to the Illinois TIF statute, and is available for redevelopment, housing development, and economic development.[13]

The Minnesota legislature passed TIF legislation in 1979 to consolidate and facilitate the implementation of TIF programs by local communities. As in Illinois and Indiana, a prerequisite of program approval is a finding that private sector development is not likely to occur, or that it will not be intensive enough to rectify the underdevelopment or substandard conditions that the governing body seeks to correct.

The statute contemplates joint effort between government and private developers and, in fact, requires the local government to encourage maximum private sector participation.

A municipality or Authority[14] may initiate the development plan. Prior to approval of a TIF district, the municipality must:

- Adopt a statement of objectives
- Propose what property is intended to be purchased
- State what specific activities are planned, listing contracts entered into, and those to be entered into
- Establish a timetable for the project
- List the most current assessed value, the estimated captured assessed value (defined as the "increment" in value caused by the project), and the duration of the program
- Adopt a statement indicating consistency with the community's general plan and the probable impact of the program on the community

As in Illinois, public hearings are required prior to final approval of the TIF plan and bond issuance. If the Authority and the municipality are not the same body, additional requirements must be met.[15]

TIF is available in Minnesota through the issuance of general obligation bonds of the municipality or tax increment revenue bonds, the proceeds of which are used by the Authority or municipality to carry out the plan. The statute's goal is to use the increase in assessed valuation and corresponding increase in revenues to retire the bonds issued and to pay all costs associated with the project. Tax increment is available to retire the bonds for a period of 25 years from the date of receipt by the Authority of the first tax increment.

The specific purposes for which tax increment financing may be used are detailed in the legislation. The legislation defines three separate sets of criteria for designating areas qualifying for TIF programs: the redevelopment district; the housing district; and the economic development district.

Minnesota's TIF statute is available in the context of "economic development" apart from considerations of physical assets. Minnesota allows the use of tax increment financing if the Authority finds it would be in the public interest, and the use of such financing would discourage an industrial/commercial shift to another state, increase employment in the municipality, or preserve or enhance the tax base of the municipality. The statute, however, limits the use of TIF in this context. It also prohibits use of TIF revenues to retire bonds or pay expenses for economic development plans more than 10 years after the adoption of the plan or 8 years after initial receipt of tax increment financing.

Ohio

The statutory provisions of the TIF program in Ohio are available to foster urban renewal in "slum" or "blighted" areas. Under the Ohio statute, however, TIF is available only for urban renewal projects undertaken by municipalities. Participation by the private sector in the development of the blighted area is not allowed.[16]

The most outstanding feature of the Ohio TIF program is that all improvements to real property in designated urban renewal areas are exempt from taxation. Improvements are financed with the proceeds of urban renewal bonds issued in connection with the TIF program. The exemption is in effect from the date the urban renewal bonds are issued until the original bonds—or any subsequent refunding bonds—are retired.[17]

The urban renewal bonds are issued under another statute.[18] The proceeds of these bonds may be used for any and all costs of an urban renewal project. These bonds must mature within 30 years and must be payable solely from project revenues.[19] Revenues are derived in two ways. They may be raised as a result of the rental or sale of municipally owned improved property in a renewal area. Additionally, a municipality may require any purchaser of improved real property in an urban renewal area to enter into an agreement, binding on the purchaser and all subsequent purchasers, to make payments to the municipality in lieu of taxes on the improvements equal to the amount of exempt taxes on the property.[20]

Ohio's TIF program is very different from the programs in most other states. It does not provide incentives to developers, but rather provides direct benefits to the end-users. The program contemplates direct action by the government and authorizes TIF as an additional source of revenue for the governmental unit undertaking the project.

California

The California legislature has adopted a Community Development Law that provides for development through tax increment financing.[21] The California TIF statute provides that taxes on any improvements to property in a redevelopment project shall be allocated to a special fund that a governmental unit can pledge to the payment of the principal and interest on loans, advances, or other debt incurred by a redevelopment agency to finance or refinance projects.[22]

The taxes on the improvement increment may be allocated to the fund until the loan for improvements is paid. If a redevelopment agency redevelops property and leases it to any person, or leases property to a person for redevelopment, that person must pay taxes on the assessed value of the entire property, as if it were privately owned. The developer who leases property may still enjoy the advantages of TIF by receiving financing from the fund to which the taxes paid for the project will be allocated.

The major prerequisite to receipt of tax increment financing is approval of the TIF redevelopment project. The lengthy procedure involves:

- The designation of a survey area for study by a planning commission or agency with the purpose of identifying areas in need of redevelopment
- The selection of a project area from within the survey area
- The preparation and adoption of a redevelopment plan by a redevelopment agency, and
- The adoption by a legislative body of the redevelopment plan which shall be subject to referendum as prescribed by law for the ordinances of the legislative body.[23]

The major factors considered in the qualification of a redevelopment project are described in the findings required of a legislative body prior to approval.[24] The most critical factor is that the project area is classified as a "blighted area" in need of redevelopment. California's definition of "blighted area" is very similar to that of Illinois.[25] Other important factors are that the TIF program will not cause a significant financial burden to other taxing agencies; that purely private sector redevelopment of the area cannot be reasonably expected; that there is a feasible plan for relocation of displaced families; that the redevelopment plan conform to the general plan for the community; and that the plan be economically sound and feasible.[26] The California statute also imposes numerous procedural requirements.[27]

Florida

The relevant statute in Florida is the Florida Community Development Act of 1969,[28] which provides for community redevelopment through the "conservation or rehabilitation" of certain "slum or blighted areas" and the "preservation and enhancement of the tax base in such areas through tax increment financing. . . ."[29] The governing body of a county or municipality must first find and resolve that an area qualifies as either a slum or a blighted area,[30] and that there is a shortage of low- or moderate-income housing.[31]

Florida's TIF statute defines a slum area as an area where the majority of buildings or improvements have reached such a low, deteriorated, and hazardous condition that it is "conducive to ill health, transmission of disease, infant mortality, juvenile delinquency, or crime and is detrimental to the public health, safety, morals or welfare."[32]

A blighted area is defined as an area where slum buildings and the deterioration of structures and conditions have led to dangerous conditions, or where any one or more of the following factors has impaired growth and endangered the public:
- Predominance of defective or inadequate street layout
- Faulty lot layout in relation to size, adequacy, accessibility or usefulness
- Unsanitary or unsafe conditions
- Deterioration of site or other improvements
- Tax or special assessment delinquency exceeding the fair value of the land
- Diversity of ownership or defective or unusual conditions of title which prevent the free alienability of land within the deteriorated or hazardous area[33]

The prerequisites for a blighted area may also be met where streets, parking, and other transportation facilities are inadequate for the current or planned needs of the proposed community development area.[34]

Following the adoption of a resolution designating an area as either a slum or blighted, the appropriate municipal or county governing bodies, or a community development agency authorized under the Act, is empowered to develop a community redevelopment plan and project, and to use tax increment financing for the project.[35]

Public hearings precede the community redevelopment plan. The community redevelopment plan sets forth a program and reasons for the redevelopment. It must detail costs, methods of payment and financing, applicable general land uses under the project, and must provide for retention and replacement of housing, including low- and moderate-income housing.[36]

Following the authorization of a community redevelopment plan and the subsequent bond issue, a redevelopment trust fund is created in which the tax allocation funds are held to finance the development plan.[37] The funds deposited in the trust are then applied to cover the costs related to financing the project, including the payment of bond principal and interest. The allowable reimbursable costs are similar to those allowable under the Illinois statute.

Footnotes

1. Ind. Code 36-7-14 (1981).
2. *Id* at 36-7-14-12(2).
3. *Id* at 36-7-14-15-(a)(1).
4. *Id* at 36-7-14-15-(a)(3).
5. *Hawley v. South Bend Department of Redevelopment*, 383 N.E.2d 333, (1978).
6. *Id* at 383 N.E.2d at 337.
7. *Id* at 282 N.E.2d at 338.
8. Ind. Code 36-7-14-18-20.
9. *Id* at 36-7-14-22(b).
10. *Id* at 36-7-14-22-(f).
11. *Id* at 36-7-14-28.
12. *Id* at 36-7-14-27 ch. 18.
13. Minn. Stat. 273.73 (10-12) (1979).
14. As defined in ch. 18, 273.73 (2).
15. *Id* at ch. 18, 273.74 (3).
16. Ohio Rev. Code Ann. 725.01 (1985).
17. *Id* at 725.01-725.01.
18. *Id* at 725.03-725.11
19. *Id* at 725.07 to 725.09.
20. *Id* at 725.04.
21. Cal Rev. & Tax Code 33000-33999 (West 1973; Supp. 1985).
22. *Id* at 33670.
23. *Id* at 33310-33370.
24. Cal. Rev. Code 33367.
25. Cal. Rev. & Tax Code 33030-33039.
26. *Id* at 33367.
27. *Id* at 33674.5
28. Fla. Stat. Ann. 163.33-163.445 (West 1972, Supp. 1985).
29. *Id* at 163.330.
30. *Id* at 163.340 (7) and (8).
31. *Id* at 163.335.
32. *Id* at 163.340(7).
33. *Id* at 163.340(8)(9).
34. *Id* at 163.340(8)(b).
35. *Id* at 163.356.
36. *Id* at 163.360-163.362.
37. *Id* at 163.387.

Appendix 7-B
Details of the Limitations on Qualified Redevelopment Bonds [TIF bonds] as specified in the Tax Reform Act of 1986

The Tax Reform Act of 1986 (the "Act") substantially reduced the ability of municipalities to issue tax-exempt bonds to finance TIF programs. However, it should be emphasized that many of the restrictions described below do not apply to bonds that are used to finance governmental facilities such as street lighting, paving, and sidewalks.

To be classified as a qualified redevelopment bond (and thus pass the first hurdle to tax-exempt classification), the bond must be part of an issue in which:

(1) 95 percent or more of the net proceeds are to be used for redevelopment purposes in a locally designated blighted area (see below); and
(2) the payment of principal and interest is secured—
    (a) primarily by taxes of general applicability imposed by a general purpose governmental unit; or
    (b) by a pledge of incremental property tax revenues reserved, to the extent necessary, for debt service on the issue.

Additionally, no fees or other charges may be imposed on owners or users of property in the designated area if owners or users of other comparable property are not similarly subject to such fees and charges.

Moreover, the Act restricts qualified redevelopment bonds to the following purposes:

(1) To acquire real property in a designated blighted area, provided that the acquiring governmental unit has the power to exercise eminent domain with respect to the real property in the area;
(2) To clear and prepare land in the designated blighted area for redevelopment;
(3) To rehabilitate the real property acquired as above provided or otherwise owned by a governmental unit (such as property acquired by tax foreclosure);
(4) To relocate occupants of structures on the acquired real property.

If a governmental entity acquires real property, such property may be (but need not be) transferred to a nongovernmental person. Any such transfer, however, must be at fair market value.

In addition to the requirements imposed on the issue and proceeds of the bonds, the Act sets forth certain requirements that must be satisfied for an area to qualify as a "blighted area":

(1) There must be a state law that authorizes the issuance of bonds to redevelop blighted areas.
(2) The governmental unit that has jurisdiction must have adopted a redevelopment plan prior to the issuance of any bonds.
(3) The *aggregate* blighted areas designated by a local governmental unit may not contain real property the assessed value of which exceeds 20 percent of the assessed value of all real property located within the jurisdiction of such governmental unit.
(4) Either—
    (a) the area is composed of at least 100 "compact and contiguous" acres; or
    (b) the area is composed of between 10 and 100 "compact and contiguous" acres and no more than 25 percent of the bond-financed land in the area is to be provided to any one person or related persons.

Certain provisions allow some earlier designated blighted areas to be "grandfathered in."

Finally, the Act treats qualified redevelopment bonds as tax-exempt private activity bonds and subjects such bonds to the rules applicable to private activity bonds, including volume limitations imposed on the states and certain use restrictions applicable to small-issue bonds. There are, however, certain exceptions to generally applicable restrictions, including those provisions addressing rental and owner-occupied housing.

Although the failure of such bonds to qualify for tax-exempt status is not necessarily fatal to a TIF project, the developer may have difficulty convincing a municipality to support a TIF program if the bonds that the municipality will subsequently issue will be taxable. The developer considering applying for a TIF program should consult a tax attorney in the early stages of his/her planning process.

Appendix 8-A
Application for a Land Acquisition and Development Loan

ILLINOIS SERVICE CORPORATION

STANDBY FEE _____
APPROVED _____
FOR FIRST USE ONLY

APPLICATION

Date: _____
Project Name _____ City and State _____
Principals _____

Address & Phone _____

SITE

Location _____ (streets)
City _____ State _____
Dis./dir. from major city _____ mi. _____ dir. _____ city
No. acres _____
Present Owner _____
Time for purchase _____
Purchase price $ _____
Terms and conditions of purchase _____

Land cost per unit $ _____
Mortgage held by _____
Mtg. amount $ _____ Will lender subordinate? _____
Details _____
Present zoning _____ Dwelling units per acre _____
Zoning does/does not permit planned use. If variance or zoning change required, explain on attachment.
Terrain _____

Cost to install per unit

Sanitary sewers   on site _____ $_____
                  off site _____ _____
Public water _____ _____
Gas _____ _____
Electricity _____ _____
Curbs & gutters _____ _____
Sidewalks _____ _____
Streets _____ _____
Other (specify) _____ _____

Estimated total development cost .... $_____
Per unit including all above .... $_____

PROPOSED IMPROVEMENTS

No. of dwelling units _____ No. of buildings _____
Type (detached, townhouse, etc.) _____

No. units (by type)	No. bedrooms	No. baths	Sq. ft	Proposed price
_____	_____	_____	_____	_____
_____	_____	_____	_____	_____
_____	_____	_____	_____	_____
_____	_____	_____	_____	_____

Basements _____ Included ☐ Optional ☐ Garages _____ Included ☐ Optional ☐ 1 car ☐ 2 car ☐
Equipment to be included in unit _____
Type of heat _____ Air conditioning _____
Other equipment _____

Amenities & when to be built _____

Proposed form of ownership (fee simple, fee simple w/homeowners association, condominium) _____

Description of any common property and charges _____
_____
_____

Project status _____
Estimated date for project start _____
Proposed financing (conventional, FHA/VA, state agency, etc.) _____
_____ Status _____

PROPOSAL

100% financial requirements: Describe amount, use and approximate timing of capital required and indicate total potential profits of projects.:
_____
_____
_____
_____
_____
_____
_____

DEVELOPER
(General contractor (if different from principal)
_____
_____
_____
_____

ATTACHMENTS
*Indicates exhibits which must be attached to initial proposal—
be as detailed as possible.

*Map showing	☐ property location arrow and mileage to major city
	☐ convenience & major shopping
	☐ elementary, junior high, and high schools
	☐ public transportation
	☐ employment
	☐ location of comparables (by number)
*E.P.A. Reports/Approval	☐ (if available)
*Plat of property	☐ zoning plat and ordinance
Topo	☐ (if available)
*Photos	☐ Streetscape photos of each abutting street and of adjacent areas
	☐ Aerial photo (if available)
*Plans	☐ (to extent available at time of submission)
*Market Data	☐ Land comparables
	☐ Product comparables—location, starting date, sales prices, number of units sold, absorption data
*Personal Resume	☐ List and description of projects developed and type of financing employed with listing of lender and mortgage bankers.
*Financial statements	☐ Current, both corporate and personal
Financial statements	☐ Five years, both corporate and personal

*Personal and corporate bank references
*Trade references
  Detailed cost breakdown
  Project development timetable—major events
  Projected sales for life of project
  Preliminary cash flow by quarter
Submitted by:
Signature _____
Name (PRINTED) _____
Title _____
Firm _____
Street _____
City, state, zip _____
Date _____

More Land Development Books From NAHB

**To order, call toll free
(800) 368-5242, ext. 463
Monday through Friday, 9 a.m.–5 p.m.
Eastern Time**

Or use the order form on page 134

To order, call toll free (800) 368-5242, ext. 463

LAND BUYING CHECKLIST

Looking for a convenient and comprehensive way to evaluate land? With this handy checklist, you'll ask all the questions vital to your investment. Just fill in the blanks and you'll have the information you need to make a wise decision. Use this checklist again and again to analyze physical features, market area, and ultimate value. Also covers escrow and title, existing liens, utilities, government requirements, and subdivision costs. 36 pp.
Members $8, nonmembers $10.

HIGHER DENSITY HOUSING: Planning, Design, Marketing

Your complete guide to higher density development.

Today's higher density boom offers opportunities you won't want to miss! Capitalize on the savings in land and construction costs with this inclusive, step-by-step guide to well-designed, quality-built higher density housing. More than a picture book, more than a text on land use, it offers a total understanding of what it takes to succeed in higher density today. Zero lot line, patio homes, duplexes, triplexes, fourplexes, townhouses, and garden apartments are discussed in depth.

In the **Planning** section, you'll learn how to shape your community's attitudes, research your market, get the approvals you need.

In **Design**, you'll examine the various housing types (both attached and detached) to determine the best design solution for your particular site.

Under **Marketing**, expert marketer Sandy Goodkin shows you how to devise and implement a successful marketing plan.

Higher Density Housing is liberally illustrated with 115 photographs, plans, sample charts, and forms. The book also contains a glossary and bibliography. 156 pp.
Members $18, nonmembers $22.50.

New Edition! COST EFFECTIVE SITE PLANNING: Single-Family Development

Today's consumers want high quality housing at reasonable prices — and that means higher densities. This newly revised and updated best seller shows how to develop communities at higher densities while conserving energy and maintaining economy, privacy, and aesthetic appeal.

Features the latest on development costs per unit for various types of attached and detached homes, as well as cost comparisons and summaries. Contains 25 site plans with techniques and criteria for developing single-family homes at densities of approximately 3 to 9 homes per acre. Covers single-family housing types and standards, site development alternatives, and community and neighborhood development.

These techniques have proved successful in communities of all sizes or price ranges. Try them for your next project! 144 pp.
Members $18, nonmembers $22.50.

Videotape Series
LAND DEVELOPMENT ALTERNATIVES: A Key to Affordable Housing

This three-part series was produced with the NAHB Regulatory Reform Task Force as part of a comprehensive program to revise local land development standards. Viewed as a series or independently, the three videos give arguments for higher density, cost-effective alternatives in street design, and practical methods of stormwater management. Excellent for showing to public officials.

Set: Members purchase $60, 2-week rental $40;
   nonmembers purchase only $75.
Each: Members purchase $40, 2-week rental $15;
   nonmembers purchase only $50.

Higher Density: Cost Effective and Affordable
Eloquently presents arguments for increased density. Includes examples of higher density single-family housing. 15 min.

Practical Stormwater Management
Discusses practical, cost-effective methods for managing stormwater. 15 min.

Street Design Alternatives
Shows how to lower development costs with reduced street rights-of-way and pavement widths, rolled curbs, eliminating sidewalks, and other cost-saving street design features. 15 min.

To order, call toll free (800) 368-5242, ext. 463

COMMUNITY APPLICATIONS OF DENSITY, DESIGN AND COST

Build for today's home buyers with this useful book. Shows you how to save customers money without sacrificing quality by using innovative products and design techniques. Offers tips on how to streamline governmental review and modify outdated development regulations and standards. 37 illustrations and photos, index. 39 pp.
Members $10, nonmembers $12.50.

PLANNING FOR HOUSING: Development Alternatives for Better Environments

How can you build housing and at the same time conserve energy, protect the environment, and stabilize costs? This book offers guidelines and practical examples to builders, developers, planners, architects, and government officials concerned with building better communities. Winner of the Special Honor Award from the American Society of Landscape Architects. 145 illustrations. 106 pp.
Members $19, nonmembers $23.75.

HOW TO WIN AT THE ZONING TABLE

Today's builder/developer must know how to work with the community — from adjacent property owners to the local zoning board — throughout the development process. This timely book outlines local community concerns about the quality and value of the proposed project, its impact on traffic and the surrounding neighborhood, and its appearance. Offers proven communication strategies to help you overcome local objections and **win** at the zoning table.
30 illustrations. 42 pp.
Members $10, nonmembers $12.50.

COMMUNITY DESIGN GUIDELINES: Responding to a Changing Market

The housing industry is a barometer of change — in design, in the profile of the consumer, in public policy, and in the economy of the nation as a whole. This book identifies the trends to watch and provides hard facts and design solutions to help you respond effectively to those trends. 58 plans and photographs. 52 pp.
Members $11, nonmembers $13.75.

RESIDENTIAL WASTEWATER SYSTEMS

Wastewater disposal is a basic concern of every home builder and developer. Use this manual as your guide to design, install, operate, and maintain an onsite disposal system. Covers wastewater characteristics, segregation, and flow reduction; site selection factors; design criteria for septic tank systems; modified soil absorption systems; mounds; evapotranspiration; aerobic units; and discharging systems. 47 illustrations, 55 tables. 110 pp.
Members $14, nonmembers $17.50.

SECURITY AND MATERIAL CONTROLS ON THE JOB SITE

Secure your job site and materials from thieves, vandals, and vagrants. Theft on construction projects costs the industry $2 million each year. Written by an expert in the security field, this book offers common sense approaches that cost little to implement. Don't accept theft as a fact of life; cut losses and increase profits by securing your job site. 10 illustrations. 36 pp.
Members $7, nonmembers $9.

FIRE SEPARATION REQUIREMENTS FOR ATTACHED SINGLE FAMILY HOMES (Townhouses)

Take the confusion out of meeting firewall requirements. Learn which firewalls and related constructions the major model codes accept. This book covers the requirements for conventional townhouses and detached homes built on or near property line. Includes an appendix of tested firewall assemblies and sound transmissions for specific assemblies. Fully illustrated. 35 pp.
Members $8, nonmembers $10.

ORDER FORM

Return order form to —
NAHB Bookstore Orders
15th and M Streets NW
Washington, DC 20005

Quantity	Title	Member	Non-Member	Total
Books				
____	Community Applications of Density, Design and Cost (159-1)	$10.00	$12.50	_____
____	Community Design Guidelines (229-6)	11.00	13.75	_____
____	Cost Effective Site Planning (270-9)	18.00	22.50	_____
____	Fire Separation Requirements for Attached Single Family Homes (277-6)	8.00	10.00	_____
____	Higher Density Housing (271-7)	18.00	22.50	_____
____	How To Win at the Zoning Table (230-X)	10.00	12.50	_____
____	Land Buying Checklist (243-1)	8.00	10.00	_____
____	Planning for Housing (074-9)	19.00	23.75	_____
____	Security and Material Controls on the Job Site (284-9)	7.00	9.00	_____
____	Residential Wastewater Systems (040-4)	14.00	17.50	_____

Videotapes

Check format desired: ☐ VHS ☐ Beta ☐ 3/4 inch

____	Land Development Alternatives (3-tape series, 222-9)	$60.00	$75.00	_____
____	2-week rental	40.00	—	_____
____	Higher Density (223-7)	40.00	50.00	_____
____	2-week rental	15.00	—	_____
____	Practical Stormwater Management (225-3)	40.00	50.00	_____
____	2-week rental	15.00	—	_____
____	Street Design Alternatives (224-5)	40.00	50.00	_____
____	2-week rental	15.00	—	_____

Subtotal _____
DC residents add 6% sales tax _____
Handling $2.50
Total _____

Order by phone toll-free!

Call (800) 368-5242, ext. 463

Monday through Friday, 9:00 a.m. to 5:00 p.m., eastern time. (Credit card orders only.)

NAME/TITLE _____ (Please print)
COMPANY _____
STREET ADDRESS _____
CITY/STATE/ZIP _____
(_____)_____
TELEPHONE

☐ NAHB member number _____
(must be included for member discount price)
☐ Nonmember

Method of payment:
☐ Check or money order enclosed (payable to NAHB)
☐ MasterCard ☐ Visa ☐ Choice

CARD NUMBER/EXPIRATION DATE _____

SIGNATURE _____

Type of Business:
☐ Single-family builder (BS) ☐ Architect/planner (AA)
☐ Multifamily builder (BM) ☐ Banker/lender (AF)
☐ Light commercial builder (BC) ☐ Real estate agent (AR)
☐ Remodeler (BR) ☐ Dealer/supplier (AD)
☐ Other _____

NAHB Bookstore

National Association of Home Builders
15th and M Streets NW
Washington, DC 20005

FINL